Bella Brum

Doreen Hopwood
&
Margaret Dilloway

Published in 1996 by Birmingham City Council, Department of Leisure and Community Services, Libraries and Learning Division, Central Library, Chamberlain Square, Birmingham B3 3HQ.

Copyright ©   Doreen Hopwood & Margaret Dilloway
Birmingham City Council

Doreen Hopwood and Margaret Dilloway have asserted their right under the Copyright, Design and Patents Act, 1988 to be identified as the authors of this work.

All rights reserved. No part of this publication may be reproduced, stored in a retrieval system or transmitted in any form or by any means, electronic, mechanical, photocopying, recording or otherwise, without the prior permission of the copyright holder.

Intellectual property rights in illustrative material in this publication remain the property of those to whom ownership has been attributed.

All photographs, unless indicated otherwise, are the property of Birmingham City Council.

If, through the inability to trace the present copyright owners, any copyright is included for which permission has not been specifically sought, apologies are tendered in advance to proprietors and publishers concerned.

British Library Cataloguing-in-Publication Data
CPI Catalogue Record for this publication is available from the British Library

ISBN: 0-7093-0219-3

Typesetting and design by R E Hopwood, Sutton Coldfield, West Midlands

Printed and Bound by: Clarkeprint Limited
Waveney House
45-47 Stour Street
Ladywood
Birmingham B18 7AJ

John Devoti
Victoria Square, 1908

Photograph courtesy of E Everitt

43 Digbeth (opposite Meriden Street), 1909 — John Devoti's shop

Contents

Foreword vi

Introduction vii

Acknowledgements viii

Chapter 1   Why, When, How? 1

Chapter 2   Work 15

Chapter 3   Birmingham's Italian Ice-cream Makers 27

Chapter 4   Daily Life 37

Chapter 5   One Big Happy Family 45

Chapter 6   High Days and Holidays 55

Chapter 7   World War II 64

Chapter 8   Gone ... But not Forgotten 69

Bibliography 72

Foreword

Four years ago I was writing a book on the people of Birmingham and I was keen to recognise the part played by other nationalities in turning our city from an insignificant agricultural hamlet into the City of a Thousand Trades. Like my own family, the majority of Brummies had always been English, mostly moving from nearby villages and becoming prominent as market traders, metal workers and entrepreneurs. But they weren't the only folk who helped make Brum the Workshop of the World. The Welsh had been important since the Middle Ages, supplying Birmingham with cattle. Later they were prominent as schoolteachers and one of their descendants began Lloyd's Bank. From the 1840s the Irish were noticable as street sellers, policemen and building workers - and it was an Irish journalist, John Frederick Feeney, who founded the *Birmingham Post*. There were less Scots but amongst them were men crucial to the Industrial Revolution, like James Watt and William Murdock. Similarly the Jews were few in number, but again they played a crucial role with renowned tailors such as Lou Bloom and celebrated doctors like Louis Glass.

Most of these ethnic minorities had expanded in the 1800s, but there was one group about which I had little information. I had a mate called Peter Recci and I knew Our Mom had gone to school with a Micky Volante, both of whom were descendants of immigrants from Italy. Talking to Our Nan and Our Uncles I learned that there had been an Italian Quarter in Brum and that these folk had made the best ice-cream in the world. I needed to know more about these people and I was fortunate to have an introduction through Micky, who was still in touch with Our Mom. There were so many Italian Brummies I wanted to speak to but I had only the time to meet a few of them. They welcomed me, chatted to me and shared their lives with me. They included Beattie Eastment, a Volante, who unselfishlessly let me use her research; Eileen Kenny, a Bove, who was a mine of information and took me along to school reunions packed with Italian Brummies; Pat Houghton, a Grego, whose pasta is cracking!; Johnny Sartori and his sister Maria Giansante, who lent me many photos; Jackie Tamburro, one of England's finest accordion players; Maria Tressine, who met me even though she was seriously ill and who inspired me with her fortitude and faith; and Joe Mattiello, who I found had been a good mate of Our Uncle George and who is one of the best story-tellers I have met.

My own research into the Italians of Brum covered the early years of their settlement in our city, up to 1914. But that was only the begining of their involvement in Birmingham life, and it was essential that someone recorded the memories of those who lived and worked in the Italian Quarter in its heyday. I am pleased that Doreen Hopwood and Margaret Dilloway have taken up that challenge. They have made a valuable contribution to historical knowledge by looking at one group of people in a small area and by drawing a clear picture of their way of life. Through a mixture of oral history, letters, newspaper articles and photographs the two authors have emphasised the contribution made by Italians to the making of Birmingham. In so doing, they have ensured that the lives of so many folk will not be forgotten. There can be no greater task for any historian and there can be no greater reward. I congratulate Doreen and Margaret on their achievement.

Carl Chinn

Introduction

There is little doubt that Birmingham in the 1990s is a multicultural city, but, for well over a century it has been attracting migrants from both near and far. One group, who came initially as seasonal workers, were street sellers and hawkers from the mountainous Lazio area of Southern Italy. These young men brought the sounds and colour of their native land to the densely populated streets of Birmingham and eventually they and their compatriots transformed part of Digbeth into a "Little Italy".

Many of Britain's large towns had thriving Italian communities by the 1920s and, whilst that of Birmingham was smaller in size than those of Glasgow, Manchester or London, it appears to have developed along similar lines. This was fired by chains of migration as these seasonal workers settled in the area, often followed by other members of their families. The initial research for this book was undertaken as part of an Open University course, examining the reasons behind mass emigration from Italy and the stabilisation of Italian communities across Britain.

Problems in research occurred as all foreign or unusual surnames are prone to mis-spelling on official documents, especially when the people concerned were unable to read or write. It is not unusual for names of the children of the same parents to each have a different spelling of the family name on their birth certificates. As far as census returns are concerned only persons born in Italy are enumerated as being Italian, so children of full Italian blood, born in this country, are not taken into account. This makes it difficult to estimate the actual numbers of Italians living in Birmingham at the time the censuses were taken. According to a report by the police, when Italy declared war on the Allies on 10 June 1940, the figure was given as between 150 and 200, but this appears to have been an underestimation, ignoring second or later generation Italians, many of whom were Birmingham-born.

During the First World War all persons who were not naturalised British subjects were obliged to report their movements to the local police and to register as aliens. The Aliens Registers were compiled in 1916 from official documentation and contain biographical information, not available from other sources, such as the actual places of birth. A sample was taken of 2400 entries from which all entries relating to residents of Bartholomew Street, Bartholomew Row and Duddeston Row were extracted. These were then examined for ages, occupations and length of time in this country to determine the structure of what became "Little Italy".

This book is an attempt to explain why, how and when these Italians from a rural background chose to settle in built-up Birmingham and how a group of young male street sellers formed the nucleus of a thriving Italian community in the heart of Birmingham.

Acknowledgements

We are privileged to share the memories of so many people who remember Birmingham's Italian Quarter, and to offer individual thanks to everyone who has helped to contribute to our book would almost constitute a publication in itself. We therefore offer our sincere gratitude to those who so generously responded to our requests for information, and offered not only documents, memories and photographs, but wonderful hospitality and friendliness. Without them we would not have been able to reconstruct the history, colour and bustle of "Little Italy" in *Bella Brum*.

However, we would like to name a few individuals whose help and support has been invaluable:

Carl Chinn for sharing with us his archive material, and his unfailing support and encouragement.

Peter Leather for his article in *Metro News* as a result of which many Italian families contacted us.

Roy Hopwood for the hours spent at the computer typesetting and designing the layout for our book, and for managing to decipher our handwriting.

Staff and colleagues in the Local Studies and History Service and the Archives Division of Birmingham Central Library for their continued help, interest and patience.

Chapter 1

How, Why, When?

"If it wasn't for them, we'd still be up in the mountains" (Johnny Sartori)

Italians have had a presence in England since the 13th century when merchants from Lombardy, Genoa and Venice settled along the Thames and there is evidence of Italians in the Birmingham area as early as the 18th century.

These early Italian immigrants were artists and craftsmen specialising in the making of scientific instruments, looking glasses and picture frames. Their presence is verified by Samuel Timmins writing in The Midland Hardware District, published in 1866:

> Barometers and thermometers were first made in Birmingham at the beginning of the last century [18th] and the manufacture took a very primitive form. An Italian named Carlotti, and an Englishman named George Western, used to make a few frames, and providing themselves with the necessary materials, visit the neighbouring towns, and make the instruments as required.

The burial register of St Mary's Church in Whittall Street records the death of Carlo Falossi and his gravestone bore the testimonial:

> Sacred to the memory of Carlo Falossi a distinguished painter from Siena. A cultivated mind and most honourable man. He died July 9th 1853 aged 76 years.

Although there is no further reference to the name of Falossi in Birmingham directories or census enumerators books the firm of Thomas Fattorini, medallists and badge makers, was established in North Yorkshire in 1827. It moved to Birmingham in 1918 and is still going today.

Many of these early Italian craftsmen did not stay long enough to establish roots in Birmingham and therefore no Italian community was founded until the second wave of immigrants arrived in the latter half of the nineteenth century. These formed part of a huge exodus from Italy and Lucio Sponza has identified two different types of immigrants calling them 'Itinerant Italy' and 'Artisan Italy'. The former group consisted of street musicians, hawkers and plaster figure makers whilst the latter group was made up of craftsmen such as Carlo Falossi. The 'itinerants' formed the largest number of immigrants to Britain in general and to Birmingham in particular.

There was a steady increase in numbers from about 1850 until the peak was reached at the turn of the 20th century. Sponza has described the 1880s as the 'turning point' for Italian immigration as there was a mass exodus to all corners of the world during this decade. This is the time when Italians became 'visible' on the streets of Britain's cities with their ice-cream carts, barrel organs and plaster figures.

To determine the reason for this mass emigration, it is necessary to examine what was happening in both Italy and Britain in the second half of the 19th century. In Italy unification meant that less land was available as smallholdings for local people and this, together with an archaic agarian system and bad harvests, made even subsistence farming impossible for the majority of Italians. At the same time severe demographic pressure -

an increasing birth rate and decreasing death rate - exacerbated this problem, and was particularly bad in the mountainous regions of Southern Italy. This was the area from which most of Birmingham's Italian immigrants came as confirmed by official and family documents and oral history.

The Comino Valley, high in the mountainous region of Lazio (formerly Campagna) in Southern Italy, occupies about one fifth of the province of Frosinone. In his book "North of Naples, South of Rome", Paolo Tullio describes the Comino Valley as "the shape of a lozenge aligned east to west with two easy entrances, one to the west [Rome] and one to the south [Naples]". Trading was established with both Rome and with Naples and, as it became increasingly difficult to scrape a living from the tiny smallholdings, more and more people left the valley for these cities. This move was in many cases the first step towards longer distance migration or emigration to other European countries or the Americas. At the time of unification much of the area around Sora (like the other eleven towns in the Comino Valley) had little or no industry, and the population was made up mostly of illiterate peasants, living on subsistence farming. Tullio suggests that "For the poor and unskilled the only way out of a life that offered work during all daylight hours was emigration, brigandage or the seminary". By far the most popular solution was emigration.

Map of Italy

The area which came to be known as Birmingham's "Little Italy" was bordered to the north and west by Jennens Row, to the south by Fazeley Street together with the canal and railway lines and to the east by New Canal Street. What a contrast to the pure clear mountain air was awaiting the Italian immigrants. Yet it was in the back-to-back houses of Digbeth that they settled and their choice of location was influenced by three main factors:

1. There was plenty of cheap accommodation in the area.
2. Work was easy to find either in the factories which were close by or for those involved in street-selling or entertaining the nearby Bull Ring provided an eager audience.
3. There was an established Catholic community (mostly Irish) centred on the church of St Michael on Moor Street.

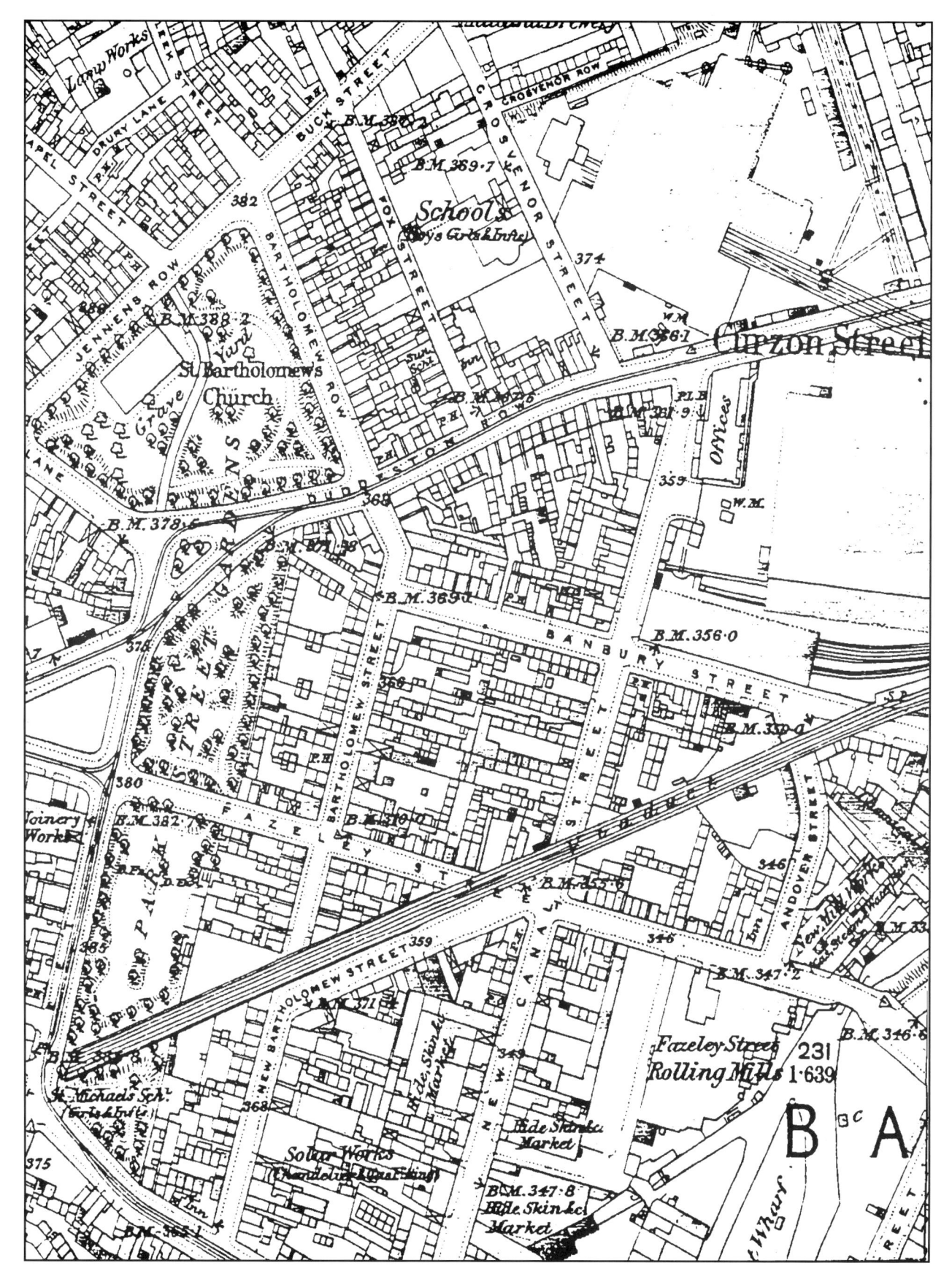

St Bartholomew's District

The church acted as a social focus for the Italians as well as fulfilling their spiritual needs, and most of the children attended St Michael's School before going on to St Paul's or St Chad's. Until St Michael's Church was licensed for marriages, most of the Italian weddings took place at St Chad's and the earliest Italian marriage traced there was on 7 May 1822 when Joseph Simonetti married Mary Galvini. However no evidence of these names has been found in local census enumerators' books from 1841. Until about 1900, most of the Italian marriages at St Michaels were endogamous (between Italians) and the registers show evidence of family members acting as witnesses at wedding ceremonies or as sponsors at baptisms.

Nos 1 to 5, Court 17, Bordesley Street

Many Italians did not make a positive choice to settle in Birmingham initially often seeing the town as a 'stepping stone' en-route to America or Scotland. Madeline Dickson's (nee Alberici) grandfather:

> Tried his luck in America, hoping to send for gran and at that time four children. He used to send money to help them, but unfortunately gran's eyesight was very bad and a neighbour would read her the letter but she stole the enclosed money. Gran and the children were very hard up and a friend wrote to grandad and he had just enough money for a one-way ticket. He almost died of starvation on the boat coming home because he did not know the food was included in the fare.

Some settlers, such as the Mattiellos, arrived in Birmingham via the large Italian Colony in the Saffron Hill district of London - the area made famous (or infamous!) by Dickens as the location of Fagin's Den in "Oliver Twist".

Birmingham's reputation as 'workshop of the world' achieved world-wide renown and, as the 'city of a thousand trades', there was plenty of skilled and unskilled work available in the expanding factories. As a religiously tolerant city it was attractive to migrants from both Catholic and Jewish cultural traditions.

Two separate mechanisms were crucial in enabling the Italian Quarter to grow and to establish itself - chain migration and impersonal recruitment (or the *padrone* system) Chain migration takes place when a person settles in a new place and as he (usually a male pioneer) establishes himself he sends for others members of his family or returns home to marry, bringing his wife to the new place of settlement. This often sparks off further chains of migration as members of his wife's family come to join them. The fact that so many of Birmingham's Italian migrants came from near Sora in the mountainous region of Campagna (now Lazio)) demonstrates the importance of chain migration in the development of the community. Members of the Volante family had arrived in Birmingham by the time that the 1881 census was taken, and by 1916, when the Aliens Registers were compiled, several branches of the family were well-established in Birmingham's Italian Quarter. Chain migration had its origins in the seasonal migrants who came to this country in the spring and summer hoping to earn enough to see their families through the long winter at home. Some of these young men stayed in Birmingham instigating further chains of migration and, along with those who returned home went word of the growing Italian community in Birmingham. There are numerous descendents of these pioneers in Birmingham today, including the Iafrates, the first of whom came to Birmingham at the turn of the twentieth century and whose children married children of other pioneering Italians. Once established in the Italian Quarter the settlers helped newcomers with transportation, accommodation and employment. In the days after unification local and regional alliances in Italy were still stronger than any sense of national

HOW, WHY, WHEN?

A sample page from the Aliens Register, Birmingham, 1916

identity and the Italians brought these with them. The sense of *campanilismo* (or 'spirit of the bell-tower') became a strong social and cohesive force. The 1915 rates book of Court 11, Bartholomew Street shows that not only were all the inhabitants Italian, but that they all had their roots firmly fixed in the area around Sora. Many descendants spoke of the strong ethnic memory of older relatives who became more and more 'Italian' as they got older - even those who had been born and bred in Birmingham! Immigrants from Northern Italy also settled in Birmingham but they tended not to live in what became the city's Italian Quarter.

Research by Terri Colpi and David Green has confirmed that each of the major English cities received immigrants from specific "sending areas" in Italy so that "... the Italian Community is not a cross section of Italians mixed up in a random way, but is composed of distinct sub-communities and sub-groupings." The immigrants to London came mainly from Northern Italy whilst those of Manchester originated from the Frosinone region. Various Acts of Parliament affecting immigration have been passed during the twentieth century, and on the outbreak of the First World War the Aliens Restriction Bill endowed the Home Secretary with powers to control the movement of all persons not having British nationality. This led to the compilation of Aliens Registers in 1916, under which all aliens had to report regularly to the local police station. In this case the Italians of the St Bartholomew's District registered at Digbeth, and some of these registers have survived to provide extensive biographical details, including place and year of birth. A sample of 2,400 entries was examined, out of which 322 related to Italian nationals - 143 of these had addresses on Bartholomew Street and Duddeston Row. This research conclusively showed that over two-thirds of these immigrants had been born in the town of Sora itself or within a 30 kilometre radius of the town. In addition to place and year of birth, occupation, marital status and a physical description of each person is given in registers as well as movements in and out of Birmingham.

Photograph courtesy B Eastment

St Michael's Church
Moor Street/New Meeting Street, 1954

Colin Holmes described London's Italian Community as being characterised by:

> ... a close-knit social life... This strong sense of community was reflected in and assisted by the spatial concentration of Italians. As a result, the community was made up of a number of economically interdependent households and this provided a solid base around which an equally dependent community life could be forged and immigrants could help to sustain each other.

This portrayal is echoed by David Green's findings in Holborn, and could equally be applied to Birmingham's Italian Quarter, where established migrants soon became absorbed into the area, whether their first place of arrival was one of Birmingham's many lodging houses or the home of a member of the family.

The 1851 and 1861 census enumerators books indicate a high proportion of young single Italian males with very few females present. By the 1870s, the male-female ratio imbalance was being redressed as female relatives joined their menfolk. The report on the 1861 census shows that out of a total of 358 Italian-born inhabitants in the West Midlands Counties there were only 66 females. However the Registrar General in the British Parliamentary Papers 1883-94 noted that the changes in England and Wales by this time "were an indication that the immigrants had been bringing over their wives and children in greater proportion ... and this apparently indicates the intention of more permanent settlement".

HOW, WHY, WHEN?

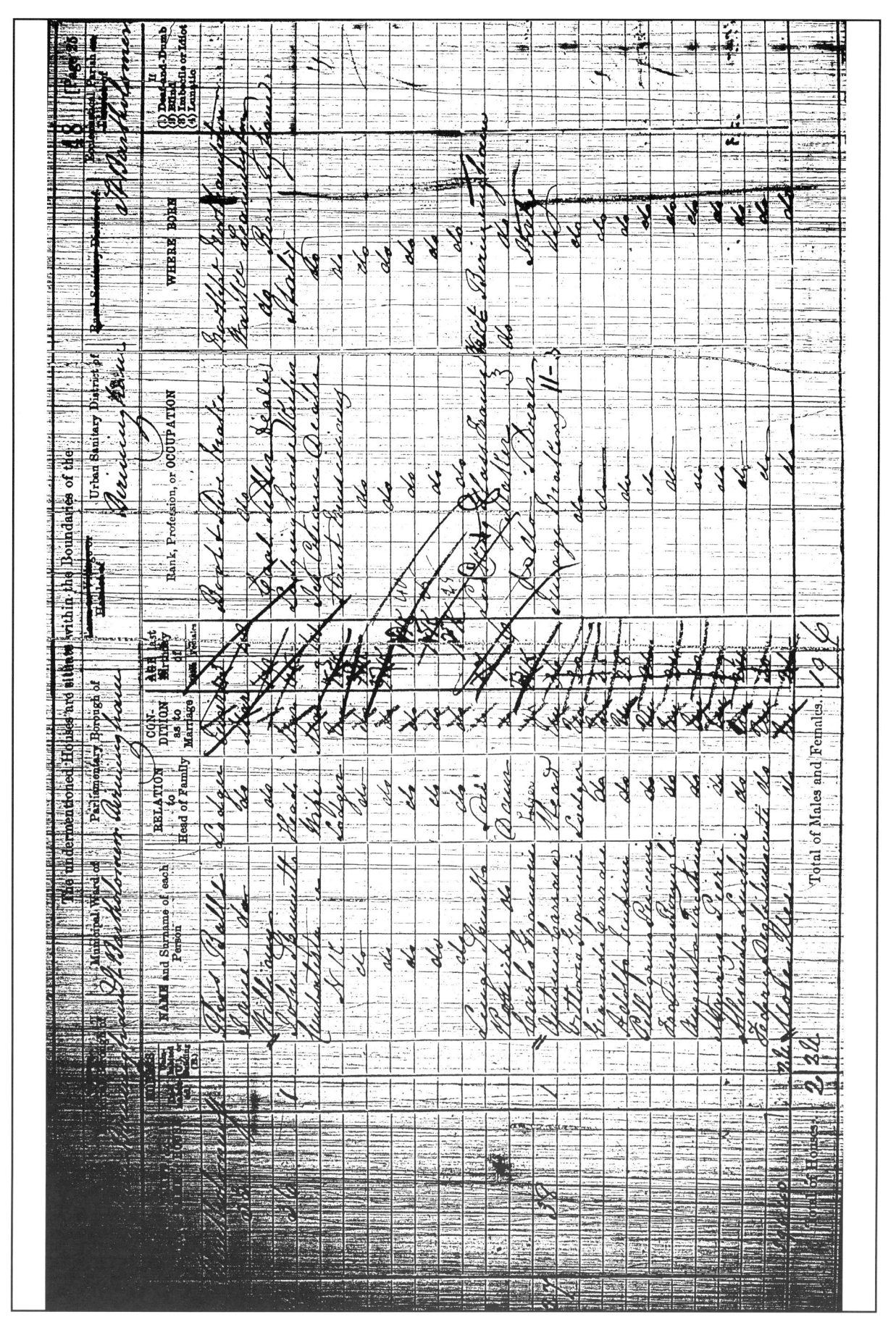

1881 census of 36 Bartholomew Street

Up to the time the 1871 census was taken many of Birminghams Italian-born residents were living in three Italian-run lodging houses in the St Bartholomew's District. Typical was that that of the Lando family who, in 1861 had 18 Italian born males lodging with them at 40 Bartholomew Street. All of these lodgers, with one exception, were single, aged between 14 and 30, and described as 'musicians'.

Communal living appears to have been the norm in London's Italian Quarter as well, and is confirmed by Green's research where "The distinctive character of the area ... was reinforced at a smaller spatial scale by the context of communal living". After this period the influx of female relatives and marriage of the young male immigrants led to the spread of the community along the neighbouring streets and the establishment of Italian Quarter s as distinct communities in Birmingham and London alike.

Impersonal recruitment, or the *padrone* system, was also responsible for bringing large numbers of Italians - usually young, single males - to Birmingham. Many of the towns' third and fourth generation Italians can trace their ancestry back to these young lads who had been persuaded to leave their home villages by a *padrone* - a local man who had made his fortune - and some are descended from the *padroni* themselves. The *padrone* would return to his native village and recruit boys to come and work for him, paying the parents a lump sum at the end of a fixed period, and providing the boy with board and lodging in exchange for his labour. During the 1860s and 1870s this system received a bad press, nationally and locally, often being likened to the slave trade.

Aris's Birmingham Gazette carried a long article entitled The Nightside of Birmingham : No 5 - Organ Boys and their Owners. The edition dated 13 September 1863 described the *padrone* as:

Place of Birth	Male	Female	Married	Total	%age
Sora*	27	12	7	39	27.3
Atina*	11	5	2	16	11.2
Caserta*	8	2	-	10	7
Arpino*	5	5	1	10	7
Arce*	4	3	1	7	4.9
Rome	6	1	1	7	4.9
Picinsco	6	1	-	7	4.9
Naples	3	2	1	4	2.8
Pescosolido*	3	1	1	3	2.1
Settefrati	3	1	-	3	2.1
Casino	-	3	-	3	2.1
St Elia	2	-	-	2	1.4
Pietmondio*	2	-	-	2	1.4
Isololata [Isola]*	2	1	-	3	2.1
Pellegrini	1	1	-	2	1.4
Parma	1	-	-	1	0.7
Trasacalo	-	1	-	1	0.7
Viaggiano*	1	-	-	1	0.7
Calabria	1	-	-	1	0.7
Carditto	1	-	-	1	0.7
Tantella	1	-	-	1	0.7
Saradileno	-	1	-	1	0.7
Castellione	-	1	-	1	0.7
Milan	1	-	-	1	0.7
Toreno	1	-	-	1	0.7
San Antonio	1	-	-	1	0.7
England	1	10	-	11	7.7
Scotland	-	1	-	1	0.7
Brazil	1	1	1	2	1.4
Total	90	35	15	143	

* Indicates villages/towns within 30 kilometres of Sora

Places of birth of Italian residents living in Bartholomew Street, Duddeston Row and Bartholomew Row.

> Middle-aged, stout, greasy (both in person and dress), tobacco-perfumed, and unhealthy looking. At certain seasons he goes back to his native Italy and there cuts a great figure in the country villages. He puts on a good coat and many rings, rattles gold in his pockets and shows in various ways that money is plentiful with him... He says "Look at me. I went away a poor lad with nothing, and see what I am now... let some of your lads go back with me, and they too shall come back rich and able to buy large houses". So he speaks to the poor peasants, and they looking upon him and believing his wonderful story, trust their children in his hands".

The tasks allotted to the new recruit depended very much on his size and strength. Small boys would be sent out with a a hurdy-gurdy, wax image or white mice, and as they grew older, they would be allotted a piano or barrel organ. Each lad was expected to bring his master a certain amount of income weekly, and the informant told the reporter that each boy would represent at least 14s (70p) profit each week. Any boy not reaching his 'target' would be soundly beaten and starved.

HOW, WHY, WHEN?

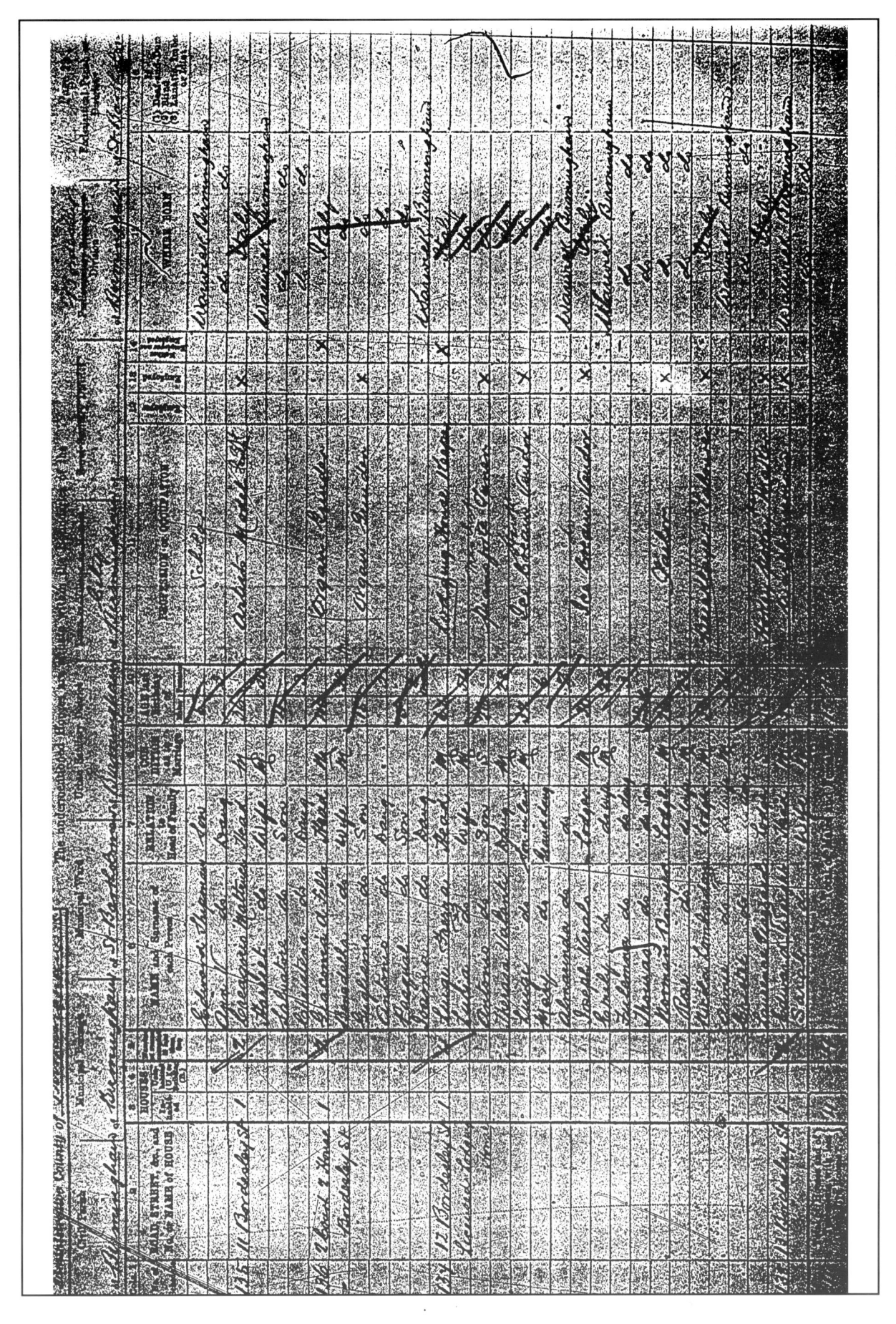

1891 census of 11-12 Bordesley Street

Provincia di Caserta   Comune di Atina

UFFICIO DELLO STATO CIVILE

Estratto dal Registro **ATTI DI NASCITA**

Anno 1863 Num. 106 Parte prima

Tavolieri Antonio

Numero d'ordine centosei

L'anno mille ottocentosessantatre il dì ventotto del mese di Settembre alle ore sedici avanti di Noi Alfonso Visochi Sindaco ed Ufficiale dello Stato Civile del Comune di Atina Provincia di Terra di Lavoro è comparso Giuseppe Delicata figlio di Giovambattista di anni quarantuno di professione contadino domiciliato in Atina il quale ci ha presentato un bambino secondochè abbiamo riconosciuto ed ha dichiarato che lo stesso è nato da Maria Antonia Tavolieri di anni trentacinque domiciliata in Atina. E dal marito Felice Tavolieri di anni quarantacinque di professione contadino domiciliato in Atina nel giorno ventisette del mese di suddetto anno alle ore ventitre nella casa di abitazione di cui coniugi.
Lo stesso ha inoltre dichiarato di dare al neonato il nome di Antonio

La presentazione e dichiarazione anzidetta si è fatta alla presenza di Luigi Delicata di anni ___ di professione contadino

INDICAZIONE
dei giorni in cui è stato somministrato il Sacramento

L'anno mille ___
il dì ___
del mese di ___
il Parroco di Atina
ci ha restituito nel dì ventotto
del mese di Settembre
anno ___
il notamento, che noi gli abbiamo rimesso nel giorno ___
del mese di ___
anno ___
del sottoscritto atto di nascita in piè del quale ha indicato che il Sacramento del battesimo è stato amministrato a Antonio Tavolieri nel giorno ventotto in vista di un tal notamento dopo di averlo cifrato abbiamo disposto che fosse conservato nel volume dei documenti a foglio.
Abbiamo inoltre accusato al Parroco la ricezione del medesimo ed abbiamo formato il presente atto che è stato inscritto sopra i due Registri in margine del corrispondente atto di nascita ed indi lo abbiamo firmato.
L'Ufficiale dello Stato Civile

Courtesy of J Sartori/M Giansante   *Birth certificate of Antonio Tavolieri*

HOW, WHY, WHEN?

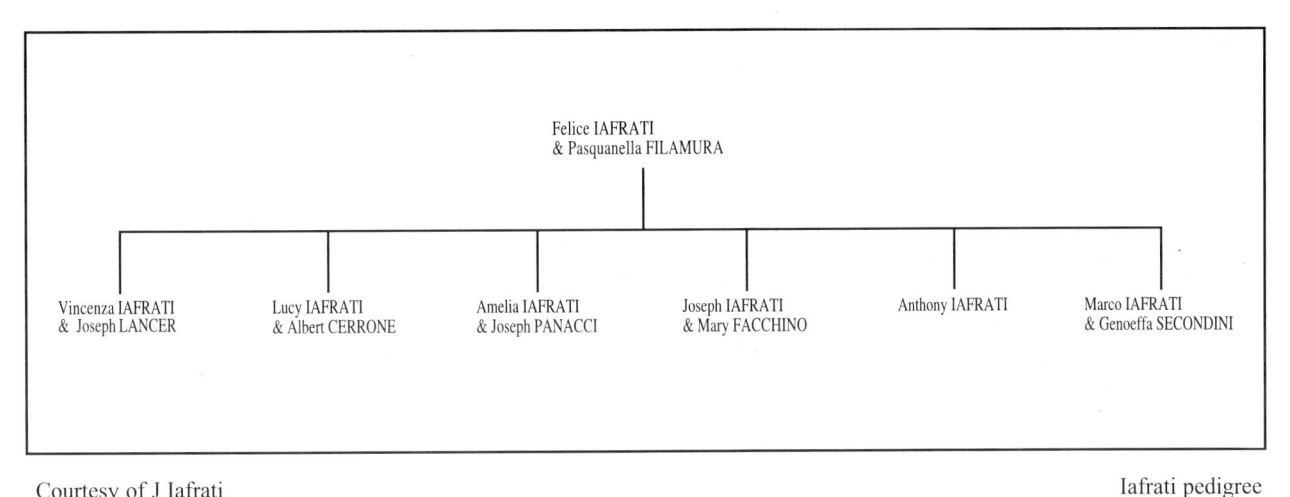

```
                        Felice IAFRATI
                      & Pasquanella FILAMURA
    ┌──────────┬──────────┬──────────┼──────────┬──────────┐
Vincenza    Lucy       Amelia      Joseph    Anthony    Marco
IAFRATI     IAFRATI    IAFRATI     IAFRATI   IAFRATI    IAFRATI
& Joseph    & Albert   & Joseph    & Mary               & Genoeffa
LANCER      CERRONE    PANACCI     FACCHINO             SECONDINI
```

Courtesy of J Iafrati   Iafrati pedigree

These large profits enabled the *padroni* :

> ... to live luxuriously until middle life, and then to return to a part of their native country where they are not known, to buy land, and to sit and smoke the pipe of peace under their own vine and their own fig tree.

The reporter stressed that his information was received from a man "who was in the hands of the crimps for more than five years", but the census enumerators' books from 1851 to 1881 for the lodging houses on Park Street and Bartholomew Street confirm that the "lodgers" were mainly young, single, Italian-born men most of whom were described as hawkers or musicians. Where any person aged under 15 was traced, at least one of his parents was also present, thus confirming that little evidence of the child exploitation which had reached the attention of the London authorities was apparent in Birmingham.

Protective child legislation in Italy in 1873 affected the employment of Italian children abroad and similar steps were taken in this country. The decline in this form of impersonal recruitment was reported in Aris's Birmingham Gazette of 13 September 1877:

> The strictest inquiries as to the existence of any organisation for the purposes of importing children from Italy have been made, but without result. Since the interference of the Italian Government, who have made these proceedings penal, no such practice has been carried out as far as Birmingham is concerned, and we may congratulate ourselves that the evil does not need any very high-handed proceedings here to put it down...

The Aliens Act of 1905 was aimed at reducing itinerancy but had little impact on Italian immigration because the new arrivals were sponsored either by family or *padrone*, providing accommodation and work for them. The coffee/lodging house run by the Sarracines was one such point of reception, described by one of their descendants:

> They set up home at 109 Coleshill Street. This was a double-fronted café with a long counter similar to those in old cowboy films. At the back was a big private yard and they kept a couple of dozen chickens. Upstairs there were seven bedrooms and stairs leading to a workshop where Guiseppe did odd jobs for a living while Maria, with the help of a couple of other Italians, opened up the café and looked after the lodgers.

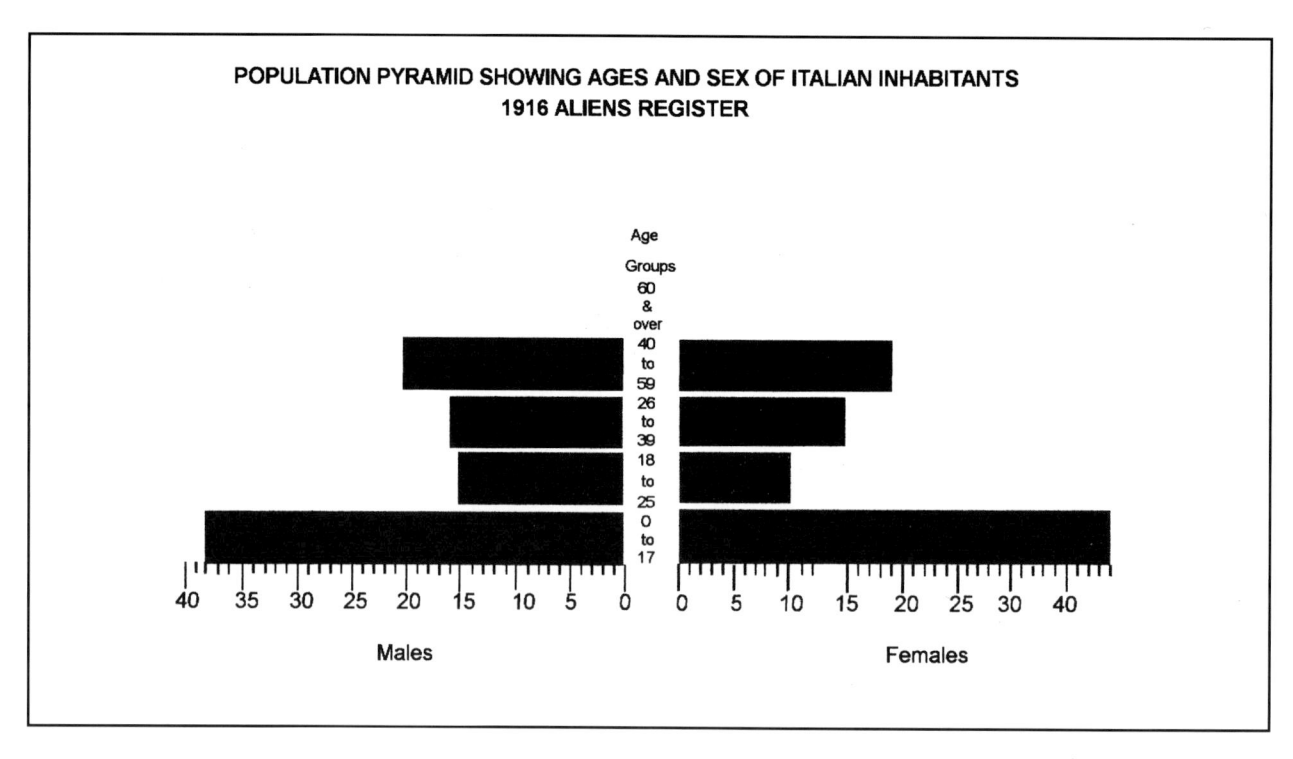

Population pyramid, 1916

Photograph courtesy of Birmingham Gazette   Hall of Memory, November 1933

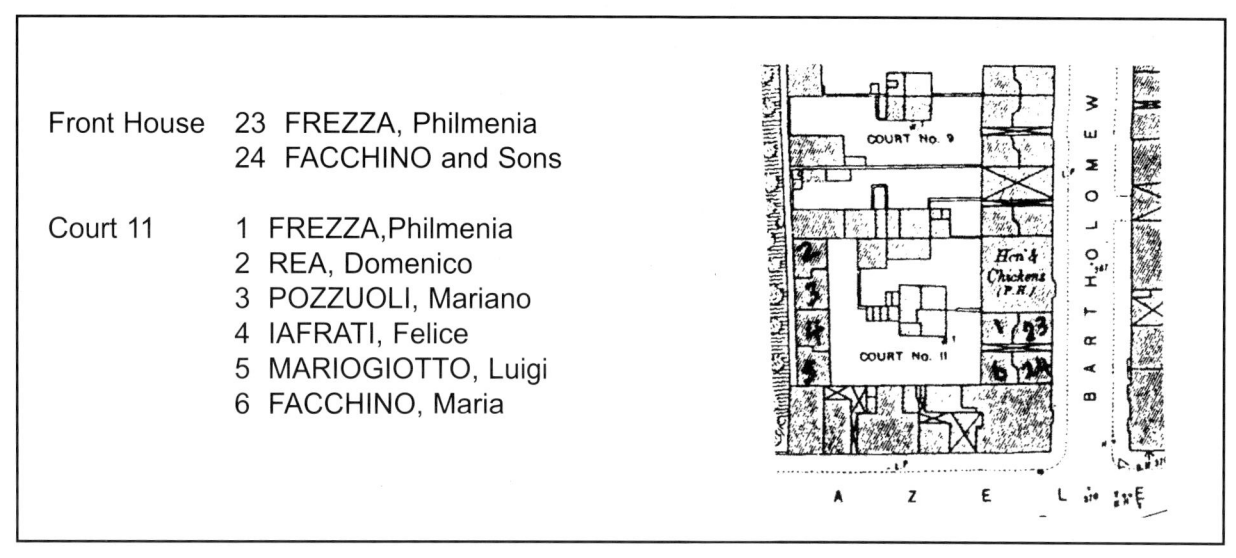

Front House	23 FREZZA, Philmenia
	24 FACCHINO and Sons
Court 11	1 FREZZA, Philmenia
	2 REA, Domenico
	3 POZZUOLI, Mariano
	4 IAFRATI, Felice
	5 MARIOGIOTTO, Luigi
	6 FACCHINO, Maria

Rates Book, April 1919   The Italian residents of Court 11 (and 'front houses') on Bartholomew Street, 1919

Although there is no evidence of arranged marriages, a certain amount of 'matchmaking' went on and where inter-marriage did not take place between families, members of the community were often linked by being god-parents to their compatriot's children.

However, as slum clearance programmes came into being so began the demise of the Italian Quarter, little of which remains today. In 1933 an interview with Vincent Pontone lamented the fact that the younger generation of Italians were no longer interested in the ice-cream businesses their fathers had established, being able to earn more 'at terrazzo and building'. The article ends with the reporter's comment that " ... the present generation living in the Italian Quarter is more Birmingham than Roman".

The early settlers spoke a dialect called *Noblidani*, and their descendants were not encouraged to learn the Italian language. Several studied the latter at nightschool but found it of no help in trying to converse with their *Noblidani* speaking relatives. One of the descendants of the Grego family admitted that her generation of Italians had at least one thing in common with their Irish counterparts at school - they all spoke with a "Brummie" accent!

Links with Italy were maintained as far as possible and Birmingham had an Anglo-Italian Society. Birmingham was visited by the Italian Prince, Don Piero Colona, in 1927 and Signor Bordinaro, the Italian Ambassador, paid a visit in September of the same year. The Anglo-Italian Society was formed to forge stronger links between the two countries and many charitable events were held to raise funds. A floral emblem was laid at the first service to be held at the Hall of Memory in 1933 and many Italian residents and their descendents were horrified to find themselves classed as enemies when Italy joined the World War in June 1940.

By December 1934 plans were underway for the demolition of properties in the Italian Quarter which, according to a reporter in the Birmingham Mail, was home to some three hundred Italians. The 'Roman Matron' he interviewed voiced her fears that this would be the end of the Italian community in Birmingham.s

Fortunately however, this was not the case, for survive they did in the suburbs of Birmingham and reunions of the pupils of St Michael's School are still an annual event at which old friendships are renewed and the kinship networks are still apparent.

Bella Brum

No. 6 & 7, Court 17, Bordesley Street

Photograph R Hopwood

Bordesley Street, 1996

Chapter 2

Work

"Work, work and more work" (Veronica Holliday nee Lagorio)

Like their counterparts from rural districts of Britain and Ireland the Italian immigrants had few skills suited to the industrial environment of late nineteenth and early twentieth century Birmingham. They had to learn to turn their hands to whichever work would provide them with enough money to live.

The young lads who were recruited through the *padrone* system had no choice in their form of work and were allocated to whatever task their 'master' saw fit. As previously shown, for most of them this involved walking the streets of Birmingham with a hurdy-gurdy, white mice or waxen image depending on the looks, age and physique of the boy. According to an article which appeared in Aris's Birmingham Gazette on 3 December 1863:

> The hurdy-gurdy boy is most fortunate when he meets with sentimental young ladies, who listen with pleasure to his soft Italian accents, admire his picturesque appearance, make sketches of him for their albums, and give him buns and fourpenny-pieces.

The occupations given by Italians enumerated on Bartholomew Street and Duddeston Row on the census returns of 1851, 1861 and 1871 are virtually all connected with street-selling - either street-musicians, hawkers or image sellers, or as lodging house keepers. A quick examination of the 1861 census of the area around Bartholomew Street reveals residents from many European countries as well as Ireland and shorter distance migrants from the neighbouring counties of Worcestershire and Staffordshire. Whilst these newcomers would also, in many cases, have to adapt their rural skills to meet Birmingham's industrial environment they did not have any problems of language to contend with unlike their Italian neighbours.

Prior to 1851 foreign-born residents were not enumerated and, in calculating numbers of Italians in the country at the time of a census, only those born in Italy are counted, not British-born children of Italian parents.

As seasonal migration gave way to more permanent settlement so the numbers of itinerant musicians and street-sellers decreased amongst the lodgers in Italian-run lodging houses. However, music continued to play a major part in the life of the Italian community and the Secondini, Jaconelli, DeFelice and Tamburro families both hired out and repaired barrel organs. Charles Alberici was taught the skilled and intricate craft of pinning a barrel by his father :

> The Barrel was covered with white paper and there were holes in it which the marker had to make from the music of different tunes. Some holes represented full notes and some were half notes. Full notes had a square pin, half notes had a flat pointed pin (called Trills).

> The pins had to be put in the Barrel with special pliers so that they were at the same height. The pin then had to be put in the barrel on a treadle lathe (Foot Treadle). The machine was erected in the attic of our house and I used to work all hours mostly night time.

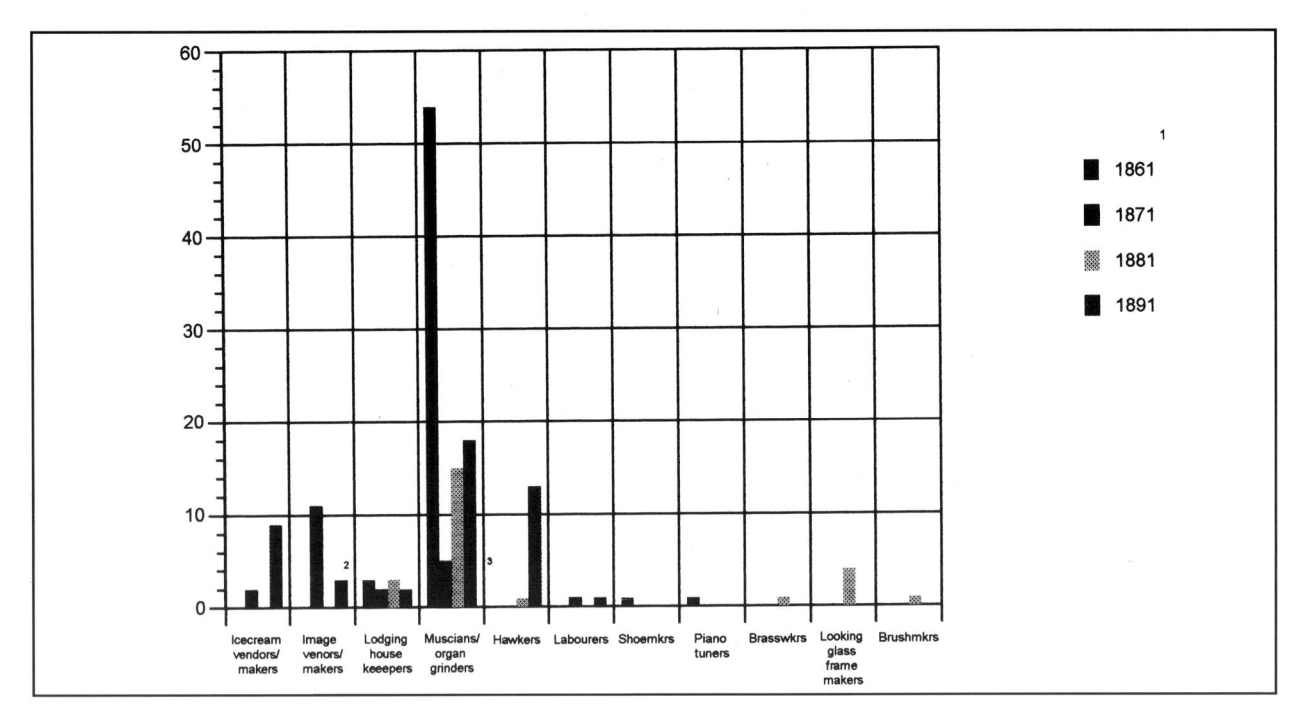

Source: Census Returns 1861-1891   The occupations of Italian born inhabitants of Bartholomew Street,

> It used to take me about one week to finish a barrel, but I got quite expert at the job. My father paid for me pinning the barrel, and used to give me 2d (1p) a week pocket money, but I had to polish my boots first before I got my 2d.

The Tamburros were a musical family who made numerous radio broadcasts as well as being in great demand to play at Italian weddings and festivals. When Maria Carmello Tamburro died in January 1955 only one son, John remained, and he swore to keep the family business on Newton Street going as long as he could, telling a reporter in the Birmingham Evening Mail: "We all lived for music". His mother had been England's first professional woman accordionist and taught her husband and children how to play the instruments, starting the children off with concertinas.

Another occupational niche filled by the Italians was that of lodging house keeper and these premises were mostly frequented by itinerant, single men staying for short periods only. The property managed by Giovanni Lagorio at 2 Bordesley Street in 1881 was an example of Birmingham's growing multi-ethnicity with residents from Ireland, Italy, Germany and Prussia as well as from all over England. By the time that the 1891 census was taken Caterina, his wife, was running the lodging house whilst Giovanni was described as an ice cream vendor.

Angelina Farina was also a lodging house keeper during the first decades of the twentieth century at Scratchems Corner on Bartholomew Street, described by her grand-daughter, Pat Arnold (nee Farina):

> My granny Farina, lived in a men's boarding house in Scratchems Corner, the end of Bartholomew Street, with a low wall at the top. The trains could be seen running along the top of the wall, from New Street, I suppose. There were three large houses on each side, all had about six high steps to reach the front door. A flagged passage divided granny's private accommodation from the working men's side, which was what granny's house was. I can see it now quite clearly, the very large kitchen, huge black fireplace and a coal fire, large white scrubbed tables and men sitting around.

The Devoti family had a chain of confectioners' shops by 1920, selling high class fruits and ice-cream as well as home-made toffee and they were manufacturers of mineral water. The Aliens Registers of 1916 indicate that John Devoti had brought several of his female relatives to Birmingham to work in the family business. Many a "Brummie" recalls with relish the taste of the peanut brittle or coconut ice which could be purchased

Photograph courtesy of M Volante   Making music in Ireland

Photograph courtesy of B Eastment   Beattie's 'Band'

Mr & Mrs Zacaroli
Photograph courtesy of F O'Reilly

from one of his shops or from the Devoti's stall in the Rag Market on a Saturday.

The catering trade was prominent in the lives of the Italians and they provided the local residents and factory workers with just what they wanted. The popularity of the Italian-run fish and chip shops, like that of the Tavoliers and the cafes such as the Brennas and Saracines, was attributed to the fact that their food was enjoyed by Italians and "Brummies" alike. Although many of the immigrants served only Italian food in their own homes, these catering establishments provided solid English dishes. Pat Houghton (nee Grego) considered herself as being English in every way, except at mealtimes! Some of these cafes also acted as lodgings for newcomers until they found a more permanent residence in the Italian Quarter.

High Street (Bull Ring)
August 1897

As the Italian community expanded so did the demand for Italian goods and services. The needs of daily life were met by the provision shops of the Ferrarins, Bastianellis, DeFelices and the Barlone's greengrocers. It was at these places that the ingredients for making pasta could be purchased and, whilst shopping was one of the few excursions that the older Italian women could make alone, they were also the venues at which the local gossip could be picked up along with the groceries. Bets could be placed at the Rapones' bookmakers and Catullos were the local boot and shoe repairers. Large or small quantities of coal could be purchased from the Iommis or from the Allchurch's coalyard on Buck Street. As well as making and repairing ice-cream making equipment, the Mattiellos ran a tinsmith's shop on Duddeston Row and trinkets and toys could be purchased from the Volante's shop together with everyday goods. In addition to shops many of the large houses in the Italian Quarter had their front rooms converted into shops selling a wide variety of goods ranging from ice-cream to clothes. Huckster's shops abounded in the area whilst others sold second-hand clothes and furniture, although no Italian connection with pawnbroking has been found.

As described earlier, specific British towns received migrants from particular sending areas, and so the occupations they brought with them were representative of Italian regions. Although the majority of plaster figure and image makers settled in Wales and Scotland the Panicali Brothers, with their business on Moor Street, were typical of these craftsmen whose roots can be traced to the areas around Barga and Coreglia. Members of the Panicali family went on to make Glasgow their home and the artistry of the brothers can be seen in the form of religious statues and monuments in the local Catholic churches and cemeteries. The Panicali family vault at St Joseph's Church in Nechells is an example of their work.

Tavolier's fish & chip shop
Photograph courtesy of J Sartori/M Giansante

1881 census of 2 Bordesley Street, showing the Lagorio's lodging house

Photograph courtesy of V Holliday

Panicali Brothers shop on Moor Street

The beautiful terrazzo work which graces the entrances to many of Birmingham's municipal buildings and hospitals was the handiwork of Italian migrants. Many of the first settlers employed in this trade came from the Friuili region of Northern Italy and, once in Britain, they dispersed going wherever work was in demand. Many companies such as Marbello and Terradura sub-contracted workers for particular sites, whilst local businesses were formed on a smaller basis in Birmingham. Members of Bacchiochi, Zacaroli, Bove, Tavolier, Di Mascio and Panecchi families were employed in this trade and the growing civic pride of Birmingham ensured that there was plenty of demand for their specialist skills.

Miss Miele recalls how her father:

> Went to work with a sack over his shoulder, with a few tools he needed. The terrazzo work used to be manually polished with a stone. It was hard and long work, using a lot of water, which, in freezing weather had to be broken off thick ice before work could begin.

Johnny Sartori's father also worked at the terrazzo at a later date by which time some of the process had been mechanised:

> What they used to do was go to Buttons to buy all the old buttons off Buttons off Portland Street, all the pearl buttons, and he used to sit there with a big bucket and a lump hammer breaking the pearl buttons up to put in the terrazza. The pearl finish.

The proximity of the Italian Quarter to the canal and railway network meant that many of the Italian immigrants became employees of the railway or worked as hauliers of one kind or another and in 1916 Giovanni Lahnn is described as a 'waggoner on own account' in the Alien's Register. Local factories provided work as well as supplying ice. Pat Houghton used to have to collect large blocks of ice for her father's business and she, and her brother Terry, referred to them as 'white coffins'. Many of the children were involved in helping with the family businesses, whether in running errands, purchasing the necessary

Photograph courtesy of M Dickson

Martin Ciangretta's (T Martin) demolition business

KNIFE-GRINDER TOURED TOWNS

Leo Maturi Made Midlands Brighter

The Midlands has lost one of its most interesting personalities with the death of Leo Maturi, the man who came from Italy to show Birmingham how to grind its knives

Forty-eight years ago he left the family home at Este, near Padua, and without knowing more than a word of two of English began to make a living by pushing his grindstone round the streets of Birmingham and neighbouring towns. He would walk with it as far as Walsall. It was a hard struggle but the warmth of Italy, which he brought to drab streets, and his obvious determination to succeed, made him many friends. Some of them are still served by his son.

Leo Maturi

Extract from Leo Maturi's obituary
Birmingham Evening Mail,
30 November 1951

With regard to your "foreign element", your correspondent should, before rushing into print, make sure of his "facts". In the first place I presume he is not aware that I have been in this city for the last 35 years, and have married an English woman; also I served in the ranks of H.M. forces in the Boer War. My eldest son made the supreme sacrifice, being killed in action. With regard to the other "foreigners", these were my own sons-in-law, born of an English mother in this city. They have served in the late war, and went through the thick of it for four years. Surely, sir, if they are good enough to fight they are good enough to work in their own country, even if their father did happen to be a "foreigner".

Personally, I feel very much hurt that your correspondent should write as he did. I am in charge of a job that is to be a memorial to those who have fallen, among whom, if the names are inscribed, will be that of my own son

Extract from T Martin's letter
18 July 1922
Birmingham Evening Mail

THE MATTIELLO MODERNE

An Ice Cream Tricycle

WHICH IS ALSO FOR USE WITH DRY ICE

    This unit supplies independent mobility and opens up a widely extended market with many reasonable easy accessibilities. The topboard, easy serving boxes and the two easily removable containers are of stainless steel and are housed in a perspex cover which is completely dust-proof.

    Each container is designed to hold five gallons and there is a storage cupboard for extra biscuits.

    There is a special cabinet with hot and cold water supplies and the whole can be kept spotlessly clean with a minimum of effort.

PRICE £120

The Mattiello Moderne

WORK

Photograph courtesy of F O'Reilly   Terrazzo workers

ingredients or serving in the shops. Whilst it was rare for wives of Italian men to have paid employment after marriage many had dressmaking skills. One local seamstress was known as Angelina "touch 'em up" Vito because of her ability to transform old garments into fashionable clothes. Others took over the day to day running of the lodging houses and Veronica Holliday (nee Lagorio) remembers the huge bowls of potatoes that had to be peeled each day for the lodgers at her father's lodging house. As well as looking after her own family of thirteen children and the lodgers her mother used to make clothes, cook for the nuns and priests at the church and do all the heavy household chores such as decorating.

The knife-grinders (*arrotini*) at first came on a seasonal basis in the winter time when farming in their native region was impossible. They would visit restaurants and hotels in the large towns, carrying their knife-sharpening tools on a handcart and re-sharpening all the cutlery there and then. The Maturi family came to Birmingham from Este and soon had several shops, the largest being on the Coventry Road. Leo Maturi died in 1951 at the age of 73, and the family still has businesses in the city today. His obituary in the Birmingham Evening Mail of 30 November 1951 was a testimony to his entrepreneurial skills.

The report on the 1891 census of England and Wales enumerates 9909 Italian born persons, 7333 male, and 2576 female. Those stating an occupation on the census are categorised as follows:

Servants	1928	Figure makers	175
Musicians	1441	General Labourers	135
Street Sellers	990	Cabinet makers	114
Sailors	641	Brokers	108
Confectioners	400	Commercial clerks	102
Cooks	278	Teachers	85
Inn, Lodging House keepers	223	Milliners	80
Paviours	176	Tailors	76

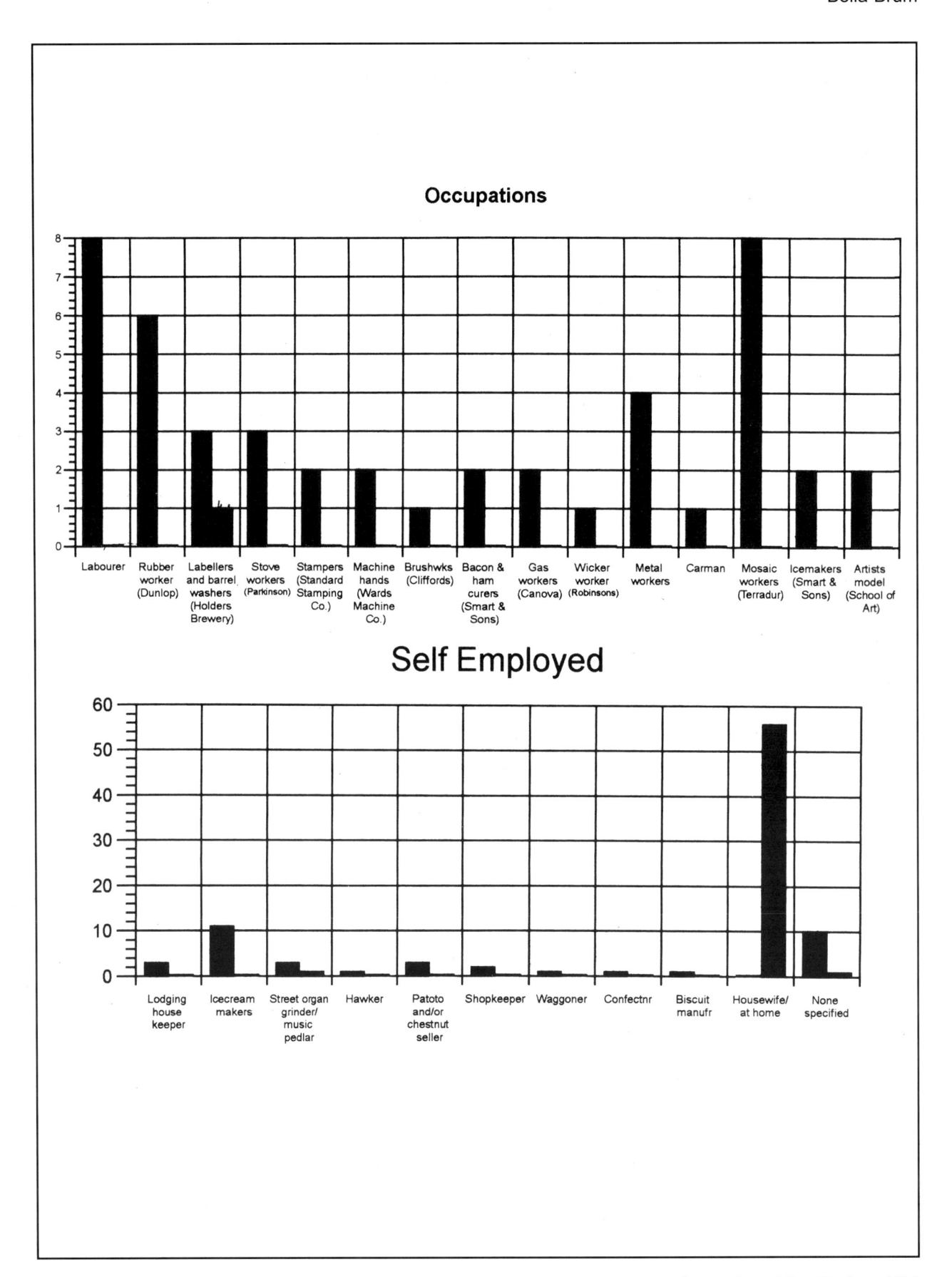

Occupations

Occupation	Count
Labourer	8
Rubber worker (Dunlop)	6
Labellers and barrel washers (Holders Brewery)	3
Stove workers (Parkinson)	3
Stampers (Standard Stamping Co.)	2
Machine hands (Wards Machine Co.)	2
Brushwks (Cliffords)	1
Bacon & ham curers (Smart & Sons)	2
Gas workers (Canova)	2
Wicker worker (Robinsons)	1
Metal workers	4
Carman	1
Mosaic workers (Terradur)	8
Icemakers (Smart & Sons)	2
Artists model (School of Art)	2

Self Employed

Lodging house keeper	3
Icecream makers	11
Street organ grinder/ music pedlar	3
Hawker	1
Patoto and/or chestnut seller	3
Shopkeeper	2
Waggoner	1
Confectnr	1
Biscuit manufr	1
Housewife/ at home	55
None specified	10

Occupations, Aliens Register, 1916

Work

Kelly's directories and contemporary maps of Birmingham between 1890 and 1930 indicate that there was plenty of both skilled and unskilled work available in the immediate vicinity and the Kelly's directory entry for Bartholomew Street for 1921 lists several Italian businesses - a sure sign of the stabilisation and consolidation of the community:

No 11		Lamberti, Raffaeli, shopkeeper
19		Purity Tea Biscuits (biscuit manufacturers) : prop: E Facchino
21A		Saracini, Lewis, ice-cream vendor
24		Facchino, Enrico, Italian warehouse
40		Farina, A, lodging house

As ice-cream making and its allied trades were the main forms of work for Italians from the 1890s to 1920s, these processes are described separately. However this does not detract from the importance of some of the less common occupations undertaken by the members of the Italian community.

Amongst the more unusual trades was that of artist's model. Gregorio Matucci is described as such in the 1891 census enumerators' book and probably worked at the Birmingham School of Art, where, no doubt, his fine Roman profile was the subject of many a drawing. This was a popular occupation in London where members of Holborn's Italian community were much painted by Pre-Raphaelites. Colpi recounts an incident in which a visitor entered the home of an artist' model whereupon all the family members present immediately struck artistic poses! The Arpini family from Atina were models for many of the French Impressionist painters.

The swarthy good looks of at least one young Italian earned him the job of doorman at a city centre cinema in Birmingham where, dressed in his smart uniform, he must have cut quite a dash with the young ladies queuing up to see the latest Rudolph Valentino film! The Alien's Register describes Luigi Valente, who was born in Picinisco, as a doorman at the Livery Street Picture House in 1916. Connections with entertainment are also apparent in these registers with numerous Italian gymnasts, vocalists and music hall 'artistes' listed as they appeared on stage at The Bordesley Palace, The Gaiety Theatre or Aston Hippodrome. Many were touring with Turner's Opera Company and stayed in Birmingham only a few days, whilst others worked behind the scenes as scene shifters or programme sellers.

When circuses came to the Birmingham Hippodrome the Italians hired out their double-gated yards as stabling for the animals and Beattie Eastment (nee Volante) well remembers the hustle, the sound of hooves on the cobblestones and the smell of their temporary neighbours.

Martin Ciangretta set himself up as a demolition contractor and was responsible for clearing the site for the Hall of Memory. This was met with opposition by some Birmingham residents who considered that the job should have been given to English workers but Martin, having fought for the Allies in the First World War, eloquently argued his case. His son in law Charles Alberici worked for him and recalls one particularly taxing demolition job where an ancient hall was to be taken apart and rebuilt elsewhere:

> It was a stone construction and every piece of stone had to be numbered when it was pulled down and the numbers had to be in Roman figures. They tried to get a stonemason for the job but could not get one in time, so I said I would do the job for extra money... I remember when I used to read the Bible, each page was numbered in Roman figures so as I went along making the stones I copied them from the Bible.

The table of occupations compiled from the Aliens Register of 1916 shows that hardly any Italian women were in paid employment and many of the men were working in factories involved in war work. By this time the number of self-employed men in the catering trade was also increasing but there were very few remaining in the barrel organ business.

Court, back of Tavolieri's shop

Other Italian families have long-established connections with Birmingham even though they either did not live in the Italian Quarter itself or had moved out of the area by the early twentieth century. Members of the Taroni family can trace their connection with the metal trade back to 1870 when Augustine Taroni was working in Aston as a black ornament maker and the family business is still thriving in Birmingham today. Descendants of the Bacchiocchi family still carry out their business on Aston Road as B & D Public Works - only about a quarter of a mile from where John Bacchiocchi kept his lodging house on Bartholomew Street over a century earlier.

Although many of the trades described above have disappeared, the terrazzo workers have left a very visual and lasting presence on Birmingham's buildings and the recently constructed Centenary Square boasts the craftsmanship of Italian mosaic workers. Football fans attending matches at Aston Villa step upon an example of Italian craftsmanship as they enter the ground, as do innumerable patients at the City (formerly Dudley Road) Hospital. A member of the Di Mascio family applied his art to the windowsills and steps of his home in Trafalgar Road, Moseley and many of the halls and vestibules of houses in the Italian Quarter were decorated in this way.

Chapter 3

Birmingham's Italian ice-cream makers

"Ice-cream? The Italians will always maka da best ice-cream" (Vincent Pontone)

Although Italians can take full credit for introducing ice-cream to the taste buds of Birmingham's residents ice-cream itself originated in China as long ago as 2000BC and was introduced to Europe by Marco Polo in the 13th century.

It is more probable that Birmingham's ice-cream makers learned their craft in Paris or even London, rather than in their native land. The Italian community of Holborn brought the cries of '*Gelati, ecco un poco*' to the streets of London and it is believed that from this derived the name 'hokey-pokey'. Ice-cream making became very much an Italian trade throughout Great Britain and some of Birmingham's ice-cream businesses originated in Devon, such as those of the Miele and Tersigne families. With the advent of cheap day excursion tickets on the railways Brummies probably acquired a taste for ice-cream at the seaside and, once back in their home town their demand for this new delicacy was filled by Birmingham's ice-cream entrepreneurs. The Verrecchia family business was one of the earliest to be established in Birmingham and by the time that the 1891 census was taken nine ice-cream vendors/makers (all Italian-born) are listed on Duddeston Row and Bartholomew Street.

At first, batches of ice-cream were produced in the brewhouses of back-to-back houses, and at Back 32 and House 33 Bartholomew Street, the Tavolier and Volante families were both described as ice-cream vendors in 1891. Members of the Saracine and Tavolier family later married and one of their descendants suggests that Giuseppi Saracine:

> ... brought a pony and trap, stripped it, built a canopy and painted it white, blue, red and gold.
> As far as we know, he was the first in England to make a noise to attract custom. He did this by ringing a large bell.

The courtyards of the Italian Quarter also provided parking space for the push-carts and, in some instances, stabling for the horses. Frankie Iommi's horse, Di, was so used to their regular route she would safely deliver Frankie home when he had fallen asleep at the reins. She would patiently wait at the front door of the house until a member of the family came out and woke up Frankie.

Ice-cream making became increasingly subjected to public health regulations, and, in 1911, the Medical Officer of Health described the existing conditions in which the ice-cream was made as:

> ... dangerous owing to the risk of contamination of the 'cream' with faecal and other bacteria.
> Hardly a single person in the Italian Quarter in the city has suitable premises for his ice-cream work.

Improvements had to be made and this led to the erection of purpose-built factories which were either privately owned, like that of the Tavolier's, or which could be used by the tenants for a payment of one shilling (5p) per week. Such a factory was built on Banbury Street where each tenant was given storage accommodation, and their own keys. The report concluded that 'The work is being continued during 1912 and the Italians are falling into line well'.

Photograph courtesy of V Holliday   John Lagorio

Ice-cream continued to be a 'home-based' industry and many of the Italian ice-cream making families had their brewhouses tiled and painted to meet the new regulations or built sheds on the premises. The Zacaroli and Secondini families (who also inter-married) continued to work in this way, and Ray Zacaroli well remembers the family involvement in the ice-cream making process and the Saturday morning rush to be first out with the barrows:

> ... it was all peaceful and calm except in the backyards where everybody was beavering away making ice-cream ... [it was made] in a tub with a freezer inside, ice around it, and it was solid You put the milk in and you had a spade. It was back-breaking work. You put the spade into the freezer and turned it. Eventually it went solid and you put the lid on and the centrifugal force would push it up, then you'd get this spade and keep putting salt and ice around it. All of a sudden you'd see all the men who were aiming to be the first out ... all these carts being pushed out of the entries and then a trail of men going to town to get the best pitches ... My dad used to walk to Lightwood Park and my mum to Aston.

Although Joe Mattiello himself did not make ice-cream, he recalls the hustle and bustle of weekends:

> ... because a lot of it happened in our yard, making the ice-cream and getting ready. You see they had their own pitches; I can remember Vincent Pannacci used to stand outside Pype Hayes Park. My mother had a pitch outside the Blues Football Ground. They all had their own pitches but, don't forget, on your way you could take a lot of money because you could probably sell a quarter of your ice-cream, or half your ice-cream, before you got there, see. And most of 'em was going down the same street, so the first one out would get the customers you see. Before you actually got to the pitch. Me brother used to stand outside Cannon Hill Park I think, I'm sure, because I've walked with him many a time.

Photograph courtesy of J Sartori/M GiansanteTavolier's ice-cream cart

The Mattiellos had a tinsmiths shop on Duddeston Row where they both manufactured and repaired equipment necessary to the ice-cream trade as well as supplying general ironmongery. Their ice-cream tricycle and the 'Mattiello' ice-cream cruiser earned Mr Mattiello prizes at the National Dairy Exhibition just after the Second World War. The new push-type ice-cream vehicle designed by Mr Tersigne was described by the City's Public Health Department in 1948 as 'the complete answer to the menace of the ice-cream barrow'. [Facchino News, July 1948]

Each of the Italian ice-cream makers boasted their own special recipe and Maria Thompson (nee Tersigne) described her family's recipe as:

> Milk, eggs, butter and sugar. Regulations came in and then it had to be aerated, so much of this, so much of that, a certain amount of butter fat. We had a proper dairy - storage compartment, freezing compartment and another where you had to go in protective clothes. When that ice-cream was done there was no comparison to old fashioned ice-cream.

All the Italians interviewed rued the fact that the new regulations had meant a loss in the flavour of their ice-cream, summed up by Pat Houghton (nee Grego):

> Italian ice-cream? Superb! Nothing can compare to it. It was different in taste to today and it had a creamy, open texture.

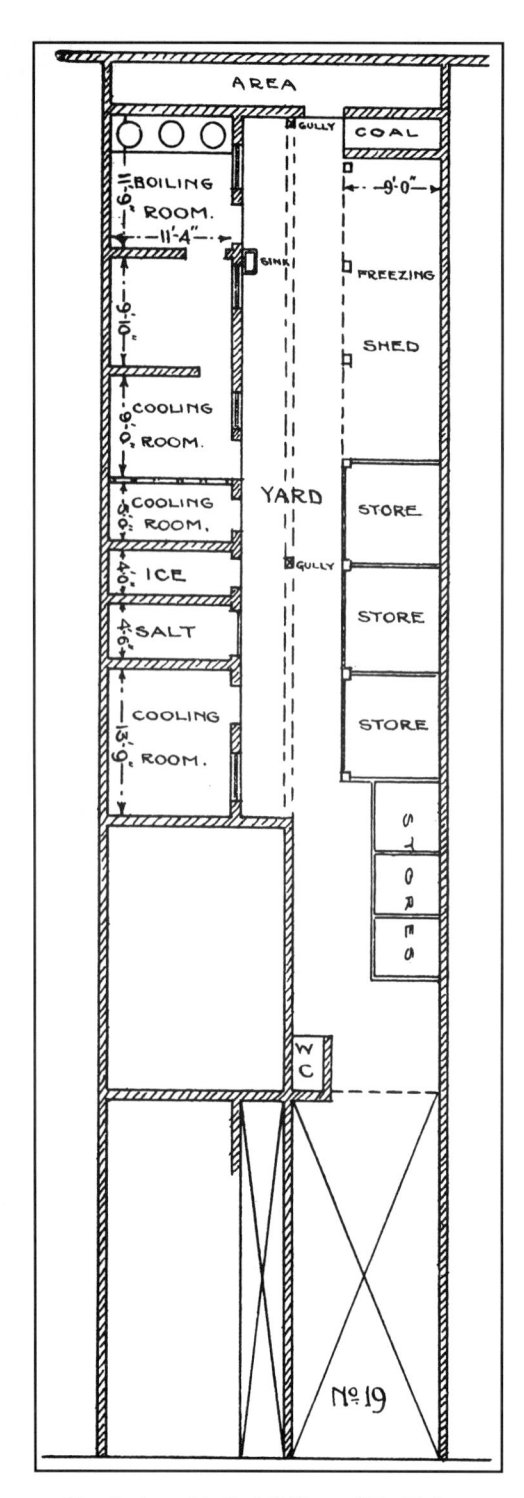

Birmingham Medical Officer of Health Report,
1911
Bartholomew Street
Plan of ice-cream factory

Gilda and Pasquale Zacaroli
Back Duddeston Row 1930s
Photograph courtesy of F O'Reilly

Birmingham Medical Offcer of Health Report, 1911   The ice-cream factory at 19 Bartholomew Street

Maria, too, had been an active member of the family business, based in Allison Street:

> I can remember as a youngster having to stand up the Bull Ring with a barrow-cart and I used to hate it. I always used to get a good hiding when I came home 'cos I hadn't brought in enough money for the ice-cream I'd sold. I can remember the stamp and the wafer-thing - which we used to buy from Mattiello's - had three notches on it. You pushed it up to whatever size they were having, say a penny or tupenny one. You put a slice of ice-cream on it so it filled the wafer. I don't know what I did, but they must've had three times the amount they should have.

When rationing was introduced during the Second World War ice-cream production came to a halt for a while. The Birmingham Post announced that the manufacture of ice-cream was to be prohibited after 30 September 1942 in order to conserve manpower, plant and factory space, estimating that there would be a saving of over 1,000 tons a year on paper and board used for tub and wrappings.

Maria recalled that when it re-commenced shortly after the hostilities ended:

> The Yanks were here ... that was our time. There was about six of us, plus mom. We'd put the ice-cream into cartons and made so many choc-ices. When they were frozen, you had to tek 'em out and cut them, and there we were, dipping them in a great big vat of chocolate and hanging them up on wire lines so the chocolate was thick around them. Then we had to wrap them up in silver paper. It was a proper production line, but all had to be done by hand ... and we couldn't make these choc-ices quick enough! As quick as they were out on the barrow, they were back for more in the hour.

The ice-cream vendors walked (or pushed!) with their carts miles every day and were 'regulars' at the Lickey Hills in the summer. Dominic Secondini would go to Bearwood daily and Francesco Grego was as well informed as any present day cab-driver with the 'knowledge' having travelled so many times along the Birmingham streets. He boasted that he could get from one side of the city to the other without turning a corner, and won many a bet by proving it!

Before ice-cream began to be sold on the streets it was usual to eat it only in cafés but, as its popularity increased, it was sold from carts in 'licking glasses' which were washed in a bowl of water on the cart after each customer's use. This unhygienic practice soon caused concern amongst health officials and the future of ice-cream sales on the street looked uncertain. Ann Evans (nee Devoti) described how her father, John, a confectioner:

> ... also introduced the cone and wafer to Birmingham which was not popular at the time. People preferred an ice-cream in a glass with soda water eaten in a shop or have a basin filled to be taken away.

As well as the families mentioned the names of Cerrone, Iafrate, DeFelice, Lahnn, Lavertine, Malvisi, Pontone and Marchione are all included as being in the ice-cream trade in 1916 when the Aliens Register was compiled.

Enrico Facchino was born in Sora in 1873 and came to Birmingham in 1899 with his new bride Maria Petricia. The couple had ten children most of whom, including his daughters, became part of his successful family business which started off as ice-cream making. He later turned to biscuit manufacture with a large factory on Bromford Lane until the 1950s. Enrico was a shoe/bootmaker in his native Sora, but successfully adapted his skills to become one of Birmingham's entrepreneurs so that, by the time of the First World War, he was recruiting young men in Sora to come and work for his business. Facchino's Purity Biscuits met the demand for wafers as street sales of ice-cream increased. Enrico opened his first ice biscuit factory on Bradford Street, and according to 'Ice-cream Topics' of Summer 1972:

> Progress was instantaneous! Their vans used musical horns as far back as 1924, and, in 1938, the first car signals obtained from Germany.

As well as 'Archie Andrews' ice lollies and wrappers depicting film stars, Facchinos' was responsible for bringing soft ice-cream to the streets of Birmingham in their fleet of six 'factories-on-wheels' vans.

Photograph courtesy of J Sartori/M Giansante — Sartori's ice-cream making premises

So good...

—that's what everyone says when they are served with an Ice Cream in a FACCHINO Cone or Wafer. And FACCHINO'S Cones and Wafers *are* good too. They are produced in Birmingham under truly ideal conditions (you should see FACCHINO'S Ward End Works!)—they are really rich in food value (genuine cake batter is used) and they are perfectly baked to a delicious crisp golden brown that makes even the best Ice Cream taste better. Everyone agrees that FACCHINO'S Cones and Wafers are good

...for you

Although FACCHINO'S Cones and Wafers are so much better they do not cost more and you'll soon find that it pays to look out for the shop that serves the FACCHINO Cone or Wafer with their Ice Cream.

FACCHINO'S

The largest Ice Cream Biscuit Concern in Great Britain
FACCHINO'S PURITY BISCUIT CO., Purity Works, Ward End, Birmingham, 8

Courtesy of A Greatrex

Advertisement for Facchino's ice-cream biscuits

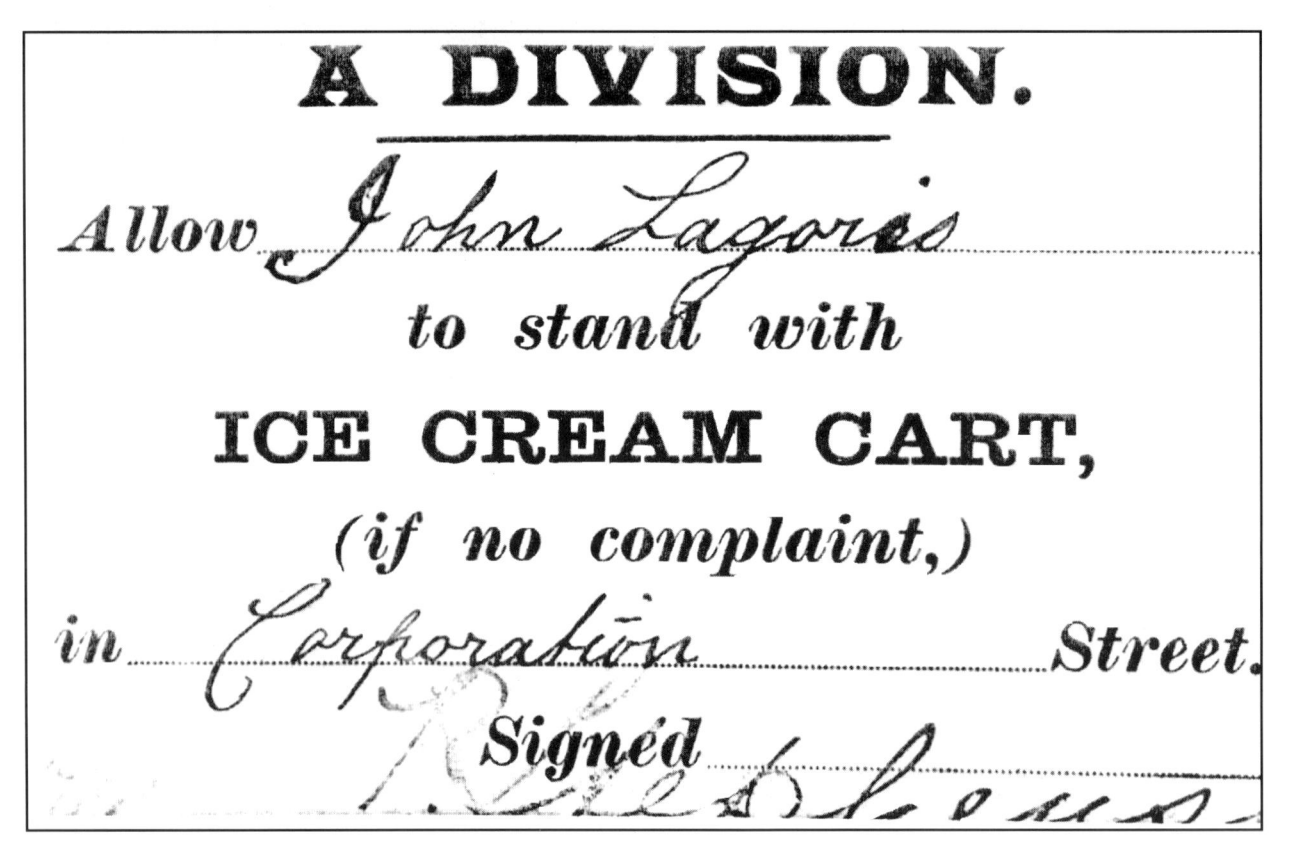

> # A DIVISION.
>
> Allow *John Lagoris* to stand with
> ## ICE CREAM CART,
> *(if no complaint,)*
> in *Corporation* Street.
> Signed ....

Photograph courtesy of V Holliday — Ice-cream licence

It was reported in the Sunday Mercury of 7 October 1962:

> Children caught on to the image of 'Mr Whippy' and his colourful vans, which had loud speakers playing 'Greensleeves' - a modern adaptation of the old Italian ice-cream sellers handbell ... Mr Whippy put his cones in the hands of adults and children all over Britain.

Almost thirty years before this article appeared however Vincent Pontone was lamenting the end of the Italian Quarters' ice-cream makers:

> Ice-cream? The Italians will always maka da best ice-cream. Da - What you call it - formula, we Italians know. Beeg English firms might do their best, but Italian ice-cream - well, I ask you. Da younger generation, dey work at terrazza and building all week and dey will no longer push da barrow on Saturday and Sunday. It is sad [Birmingham Despatch, 10 November 1933].

Francesco Grego took his recipe for ice-cream with him to his grave for none of his sons were interested in carrying on the family busines. Although his daughter, Pat, asked him for the recipe on several occasions he did not pass it on to her.

Once the big ice-cream companies' vans came on to the streets of Birmingham there was intense and sometimes fierce competition between them and the 'old' ice-cream sellers. Where rivalry had previously existed between the Italians this had not been malicious and each business respected the others 'territory'. Maria Tersigne was told by her brother to give her ice-cream away if an ice-cream van poached on her round.

Hand in hand with the ice-cream making went baked potatoes and chestnuts. Beattie Eastment (nee Volante) confirmed that this was seasonal business - ice-cream in the summer, potatoes and chestnuts in the winter. Licences were issued to the sellers for their pitches, which were either outside or inside the football grounds, parks, theatres and cinemas of Birmingham. Giovanni (John) Lagorio was one of the first holders of such a

Photograph courtesy of J Mattiello

Mattiello's Shop, Duddeston Row

licence and his daughter, Veronica (now Holliday) remembers how the whole family was involved in cleaning the potatoes which was a wet and cold task in winter, especially when the weather was freezing. Molly Hemming (nee Allchurch) lived close to the DeFelices whose yard was always piled high with potatoes which Mrs DeFelice used to scrub with a huge broom - sometimes having to chase away the rats first!

Members of the Verrecchia family are described on the 1891 census of Birmingham as ice-cream makers/vendors and another branch of this family still runs a fleet of ice-cream vans from their premises in West Bromwich. Tony Verrecchia and George Parkinson were photographed selling their ice-cream in Ladywood in 1948 and are still running the family business today although the Verrecchias no longer manufacture their own products. The company's bright orange and white vans are visible proof that the Italian connection with ice-cream in Birmingham is still continuing.

The decline in ice-cream manufacture by the small family businesses occurred partly due to the emergence of the large local companies such as Meddocream and Eldorado and nationals such as Lyons and Walls, with whom the small businesses could not compete. As the St Bartholomew District fell victim to redevelopment the Italians moved to the suburbs where their ice-cream making skills died with them.

Italian ice-cream parlours can still be found in the coastal resorts of South Wales and Scotland but, sadly, no longer in Birmingham. So ... once again 'Brummies' are getting the taste for Italian ice-cream on their holidays.

Photograph courtesy of T Verrecchia George Parkinson (left) and Tony Verrecchia, Ladywood, 1948

Photograph R Hopwood George Parkinson (left) and Tony Verrecchia. West Bromwich, 1996

Chapter 4

Daily Life

"Yoh eat worms, don't ya" (Pat Houghton nee Grego)

Infant mortality rates in the St Bartholomew's district were amongst the highest in Birmingham, as can be seen by the Medical Officer of Health Reports for the years 1898 and 1921 and these can be attributed to the poor quality of housing and to living conditions in general.

As the St Bartholomew's ward was repeatedly amongst the three wards returning the highest death rates, an enquiry was made "so that it might be seen whether the high mortality was common to the whole ward or was confined to certain streets' [MOH. 1898]. Bartholomew Street was one of the highest, with an annual death rate of 33 per 1,000 during the ten year period 1888-97 and where over half of the houses were rented at 3/6d (17p) per week and almost three quarters had no ventilation. The report concluded that "The unhealthiness of the great majority of the streets is clearly not due to their situation, but to their condition".

Amongst Birmingham's Italian Community traditional and alternative remedies abounded and the occasions where the local doctors was called were very few and far between. More often than not the 'old wives' arrived to offer advice and treatment and, hopefully, to celebrate the speedy recovery of their patient.

Modesto Sartori remembered when members of the community who had any sickness which would not go away, that a group of elderly ladies would be called upon for assistance. A saucer would be placed on the table and the ladies would pour a few drops of holy water into it and then float a lighted night-light on the surface. Drops of olive oil would then be trickled on the water and the ladies would watch closely to see if it sank to the base of the saucer. If it did, the *molluch*, or devil, was deemed to have been cast out and the patient would make a speedy and full recovery. If a patient did not look as if he or she would get better then the same group of ladies would appear to sit by the sick bed and recite their rosaries until the priest was sent for.

The memory of the night prior to his grandmother's death is still fresh in the memory of Joe Iafrati. He and his brother Anthony, were being rather noisy (as usual!) after going to bed and their grandfather shouted at them to be quiet from the bottom of the stairs. Joe remembers his grandmother replying: " 'Arry, leave them alone, they are only children". The boys were horrified to find, on getting up next morning, that grandma had died during the night and was laid out on the huge dining table clothed in her Sunday best dress with candles at her head and feet. The undertaker was a local man known as 'Old Man Hazel' and he placed Mrs Iafrati in her coffin which was left in the parlour for two days so that her relatives, neighbours and friends could come and pay their last respects. Vincenzia Iafrati was then laid to rest in the family grave at New Oscott Cemetery

Common childhood diseases, such as measles, brought fear to the inhabitants of the Italian Quarter for these took their toll of local infants and children. Babies fell victim to bronchitis and whooping cough and the majority of children in the area would have witnessed the death of at least one sibling during their own childhood. Vincenzo Volante mourned the death of three of his daughters in a period of just one year. Elena Volante died of measles in January 1896 and their next child was named Elena in her memory. Sadly, she lived only to the age of two months, succumbing to marasmus [wasting away] and her sister Celesta aged sixteen months, had pre-deceased her by only one week. She had fallen victim to a common ailment in the damp housing conditions - bronchitis. Many of the Italian-born inhabitants of Birmingham suffered from chest complaints, and the living conditions in this area were in sharp contrast to the 'sunny south' from which they came. Pat Houghton's father, Francesco Grego, had both asthma and bronchitis which were so bad that she could hear him coming from the far end of the street. The sound of his rasping breath served as her cue to put his dinner onto the table.

A young victim was Fiori Grecco, the son of Larento and Domenica, who died at the age of two months in January 1902. Unfortunately, the Registrar who recorded his birth had written 'Flower' (*fiori* in Italian means flower), either intentionally or mistakenly on his birth certificate, and this name followed him to his grave when his death was also registered as 'Flower'. He was only one of many little "flowers" who did not bloom.

Many of the people interviewed voiced how, as children, they could not understand the differences in action and attitude before and after a funeral. Joe Iafrati remembers how members of the deceased's family were prostrate with grief in the period preceding and during the funeral yet, in the ensuing wake, high jinks were the order of the day. Much laughter and joking abounded as the tension was released.

Food was prepared by the women, usually a cold collation, and wine rather than beer was served to the mourners. Death announcement cards were considered essential by those who could afford them. These always had a beautiful religious picture on the front, with an appropriate text on the reverse and were lovingly kept by those who remembered the deceased.

Children who fell ill with viruses such as tuberculosis or rheumatic fever were sent to one of the open air schools or sanatoria in rural Warwickshire. Madeline Dickson (nee Alberici) spent some considerable time at Haseley Hall, run by Frank Matthews. The weekly cost of 17/6d (87p) was too much for her parents to afford, so her father, an ex-soldier, was helped by the British Legion. Parents were allowed to visit on the first Saturday of each month, and Madeline's duly made the long journey, bringing her a fid bar of Cadbury's chocolate. On returning home she found she had brothers and sisters who she hardly knew, and was greeted by the welcome of "Oos her?".

The Panicali Brothers were monumental stonemasons and fine plaster workers with a business on Moor Street. Many of the graves of Italians in St Josephs Church yard, (in Nechells), at New Oscott, the Abbey (at Erdington) and Witton Cemetery have fine headstones and figures carved by these craftsmen. They were also terrazzo workers, employing men to carry out contracts on some of Birmingham's municipal buildings.

The Birmingham Post AND JOURNAL

THURSDAY, AUGUST 4, 1932.

MOTOR-CYCLIST'S DEATH.

RESULT OF A WALSALL ROAD COLLISION.

The death of a motor-cyclist which followed an accident on the Walsall Road, Perry Barr, on Saturday, was the subject of an inquest conducted by the Deputy Coroner (Mr. D. L. Cuthbertson) in Birmingham yesterday. Deceased was Antonio Fury Tavolier (30), ice cream vendor, 48, Malvern Hill Road, Nechells.

Harry Whitehouse said Tavolier was riding his motor-cycle combination towards Birmingham, and when near the canal bridge on a part of the road barricaded off for repairs his machine appeared to strike an obstruction and got "into a wobble," went on to the wrong side, and collided head-on with a motor-car travelling on its correct side in the opposite direction.

In witness's opinion, if the car had been going more slowly—its speed was thirty to thirty-five miles an hour—it could have been pulled up sooner. The motor-cyclist's speed was about twenty-five miles an hour.

Wilfred Nicholls, Rose Lea, Wallington Heath, Bloxwich, the driver of the car involved in the collision, said he was in third gear at the time, and his speed was not more than twenty-five miles an hour. He saw a "dead slow" warning when he approached the part of the road which was under repair. From the time he first saw the combination approaching it seemed to be out of control, and was bouncing up and down like a rubber ball. Witness expected the driver to throttle off, but instead he came on. When the collision occurred witness had brought his car almost to a standstill.

The Deputy Coroner: The indications are that after the impact you pushed this motor-cycle some ten yards?

Witness: Yes, but he shot across the road, and the impact was very great.

How could you travel on ten yards pushing this machine if you had brought your car to a standstill?—It was such a terrible bang. I did all I humanly could, but naturally I lost myself a bit, and I may have released the clutch or the brake after the collision.

"He was flying and I was crawling," witness added.

The medical evidence was that deceased died the same day from a fractured skull and laceration of the brain. He did not recover consciousness.

A verdict of "Accidental death" was returned by the jury.

Daily Life

Table V. Deaths under 1 per 1,000 Births in Wards.

Year	St. Paul's	St. Mary's	Duddeston and Nechells	St. Bartholomew's	St. Martin's	Market Hall	Ladywood	Central Wards	Deritend	Aston	Washwood Heath	Saltley	Small Heath	Sparkbrook	Balsall Heath	Edgbaston	Rotton Park	All Saints'	Middle Ring	Soho	Saltwell	Handsworth	Perry Barr	Erdington North	Erdington South	Yardley	Acocks Green	Sparkhill	Moseley and King's Heath	Selly Oak	King's Norton	Northfield	Harborne	Outer Ring
1912	134	194	180	134	136	138	123	148	102	105	97	109	85	90	81	87	112	98	97	76	87	78	?	62	97	109	79	61	74	57	80	60	87	77
1913	162	229	179	205	180	155	159	181	100	136	114	94	113	98	99	109	137	124	112	104	79	69	?	68	82	67	102	60	60	82	78	63	54	74
1914	153	195	173	167	148	166	166	167	115	138	87	109	89	102	80	72	134	135	106	89	64	94	?	104	74	83	95	75	54	70	78	90	53	79
1915	170	187	158	180	157	123	126	157	102	28	123	86	86	87	91	82	118	108	101	92	106	94	?	84	69	56	73	55	61	94	87	123	81	83
Average	**155**	**201**	**172**	**171**	**155**	**145**	**143**	**163**	**105**	**127**	**105**	**99**	**93**	**94**	**88**	**87**	**125**	**116**	**104**	**90**	**84**	**84**	?	**79**	**80**	**79**	**87**	**63**	**63**	**76**	**81**	**84**	**69**	**78**
1916	160	159	164	139	150	139	121	147	82	114	93	79	69	70	62	98	96	96	86	94	68	91	?	80	39	83	76	55	76	83	61	59	69	72
1917	115	168	136	132	112	89	112	123	93	105	96	97	94	110	83	73	93	122	97	74	37	71	?	74	80	95	75	90	41	66	77	50	44	67
1918	156	148	104	137	120	152	104	132	111	113	70	100	69	99	86	80	101	88	92	83	64	72	?	57	57	67	82	66	58	60	70	89	69
1919	109	103	105	102	95	120	100	105	79	93	90	64	67	60	64	61	97	88	76	97	71	63	?	39	79	83	47	36	44	76	69	43	79	64
1920	112	121	93	111	102	85	105	104	80	78	83	72	80	80	98	64	79	78	79	55	75	51	?	61	47	54	64	73	53	64	43	28	50	55
Average	**130**	**140**	**120**	**124**	**116**	**117**	**108**	**122**	**89**	**101**	**86**	**82**	**76**	**84**	**79**	**75**	**93**	**94**	**86**	**81**	**63**	**70**	?	**62**	**60**	**76**	**69**	**64**	**56**	**69**	**62**	**50**	**66**	**65**
1921	106	116	104	113	85	117	96	105	87	82	91	75	57	60	62	75	78	104	77	57	72	69	?	44	68	43	62	67	69	47	60	97	42	61
1922	105	117	102	115	107	113	102	109	58	84	69	82	68	92	81	75	101	90	80	66	68	51	?	54	69	55	79	56	81	69	41	58	58	62
1923	104	103	99	81	93	80	79	91	60	85	68	59	62	59	54	51	67	79	64	54	57	45	?	48	58	73	49	34	49	53	76	21	46	51
1924	87	123	103	119	110	81	86	101	68	87	62	95	85	64	83	67	85	80	77	63	67	49	?	70	52	62	50	58	69	74	59	54	57	50
1925	120	100	101	106	107	119	73	104	87	104	69	65	58	77	64	70	53	92	74	66	39	64	?	54	32	45	53	55	39	51	66	39	42	50
Average	**104**	**112**	**102**	**107**	**100**	**102**	**87**	**102**	**72**	**88**	**72**	**75**	**66**	**70**	**69**	**68**	**77**	**89**	**74**	**61**	**61**	**56**	?	**54**	**56**	**56**	**59**	**54**	**61**	**59**	**60**	**54**	**49**	**57**
1926	106	122	79	98	86	106	81	97	52	77	66	43	48	70	52	59	63	65	59	76	98	53	?	46	52	56	48	70	54	69	65	68	90	65
1927	115	115	104	81	89	85	78	95	78	80	73	64	34	73	87	66	89	82	73	81	44	47	?	59	49	66	36	71	42	61	44	45	78	56
1928	71	101	73	89	84	100	69	84	63	57	62	71	59	56	62	46	75	46	60	74	68	34	0	62	40	43	49	47	41	82	54	46	65	50
1929	120	111	125	98	108	73	108	106	80	86	92	69	50	45	51	84	82	72	71	92	46	43	0	56	49	65	68	74	38	76	54	60	58	56
1930	89	75	67	74	91	88	74	80	53	61	37	54	42	55	69	77	63	67	58	65	38	47	63	54	51	55	41	51	49	49	36	38	53	49
Average	**100**	**105**	**90**	**88**	**92**	**90**	**82**	**92**	**65**	**72**	**66**	**60**	**47**	**60**	**64**	**66**	**74**	**66**	**64**	**78**	**59**	**45**	?	**55**	**48**	**57**	**48**	**63**	**45**	**67**	**51**	**51**	**69**	**55**
1931	85	107	87	86	99	103	105	96	86	87	76	59	48	61	70	83	100	80	75	83	33	60	57	55	59	55	63	45	49	66	60	44	37	65
1932	92	105	98	77	87	76	69	86	52	97	48	61	73	87	46	63	62	74	66	95	37	63	72	56	56	58	59	53	45	47	76	43	43	57
1933	82	73	72	100	85	79	75	81	56	59	70	54	99	65	44	72	69	74	66	60	75	49	67	58	45	66	64	60	65	37	38	76	68	59

Medical Officer of Health Report, 1931

Deaths under 1 per 1,000 births in Wards

Photograph courtesy of E Everitt

Funeral of John Devoti, aged 3 months, 1900

Years before health and safety was taken seriously, accidents and fatalities were common occurrences, and reports of the coroners in local newspapers of the period catalogue incidents at home, in the street and at the workplace. One such inquest, held on 11 May 1911 reported the tragic fire at the premises of Leo Maturi at 53 Stafford Street in which his niece and daughter died. A fire had started in the kitchen, trapping his eight month old daughter, Irene, and Mary Isabella, his thirteen year old niece. Both mother and father made unsuccessful attempts to gain entry to the burning house, but were beaten back by the flames. Chief Fire Officer Tozer stated that "The room was small and the back door being open, a flue was formed which carried the flames upstairs". The two girls were buried at St Joseph's Church in Nechells.

An inquest held on 4 February 1902 recorded the death of Antonio Bacchiocchi, a bricklayer's labourer, of 2 House, 22 Court Bordesley Street. He died as a result of "injuries sustained by a fall from a scaffold at St Peter's Church, George Street West". Antonio was described as a "man of steady habits" who had been working on stripping away the wooden casing which had been placed around the arches when the church was built. One of the pieces of wood gave way causing Antonio to fall off the scaffold. He died two days later at the General Hospital without having gained consciousness. A verdict of "accidental death" was recorded but it was noted that the scaffold was "not quite complete" at the point where Antonio fell to his death.

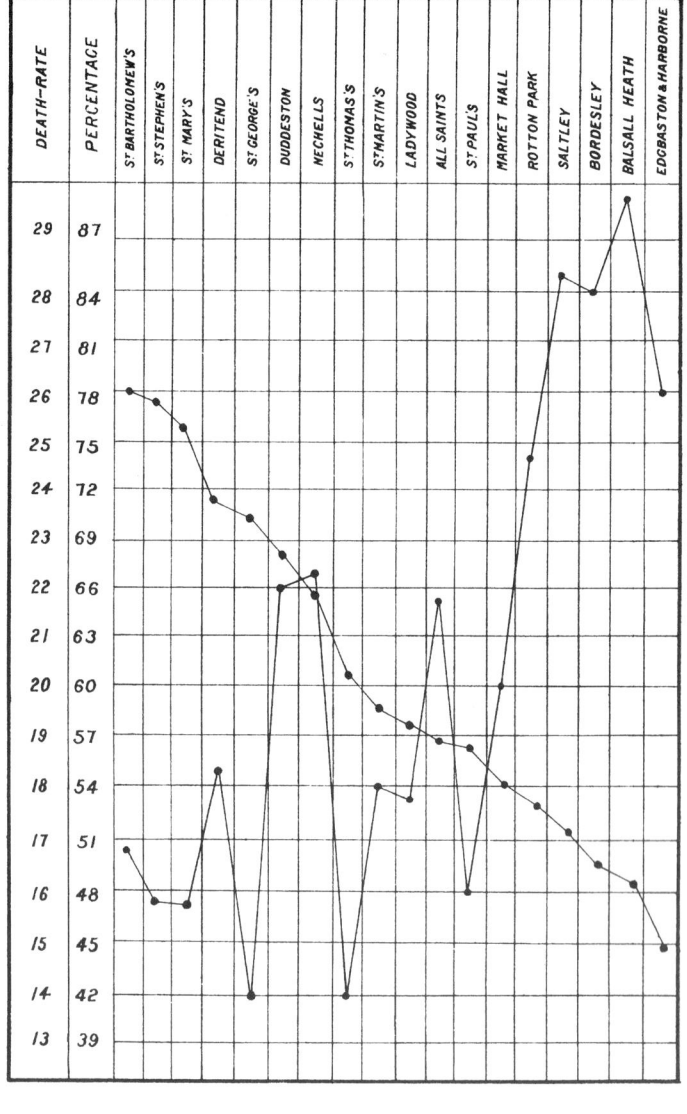

Death rate per 1,000
Percentage of houses with through ventilation

Traffic accidents also took their toll of Birmingham's residents including Antonio Tavolier who was killed on the Walsall Road, Perry Barr, in August 1932 after being knocked off his motor cycle combination. Playing in the streets of the Italian Quarter posed no such problem for the children, for as Pat Houghton stated "You saw a car about once every three days".

The Italian inhabitants of the St Bartholomew's District were ahead of their time with regard to health food. Long before pasta, tomatoes and olive oil were recognised as as fibrous and low fat they were eaten daily in even the poorest of Italian households.

Pat Houghton remembers her grandmother's enormous scrubbed white kitchen table, on to the middle of which would be tipped a huge bag of durum flour. A ring would be formed by hand and her grandmother would then toss in eggs and water. She would then:

> throw it all together with the flour and salt, her hands making circular movements until a ball of paste, 15 to 20 inches in diameter, was formed. This was then rolled out, using a broom stale, to form a thin circle and then twisted over until it formed a 'huge Swiss roll'. It would then be cut into strips with a lethally sharp knife to a thickness of about a third of an inch.

Pat remembers her grandmother's 'love knots' made from eggs, flour and castor sugar which were served as a dessert.

Beattie Eastment (nee Volante) has fond memories of her mother's home-made macaroni, but more especially the *nyuks* that she made from flour and potato and then rolled into thin sausages. Having an Italian father and English mother Beattie reckoned that as far as food was concerned she had the best of both worlds. Hungry children never had to wait long for a freshly cooked meal as pasta only took two or three minutes to cook on the black leaded grate, where the thick, rich sauce was always bubbling aromatically on the hob. Veronica's mother always had two pans ready - one of "wet" macaroni to make a sort of soup and a pan of "dry" pasta which would be served with a sauce.

Pat's cousin Eileen had an English boyfriend who was most suspicious of Italian food. Her Aunty Teresa teased him so much that he finally agreed to try some and he enjoyed his first taste of Italian food so much that he asked for more! When he told his parents they were horrified. "Imagine eating that stuff!" they retorted, "Twopence a bucket!" He even got to enjoy the leftover spaghetti which was fried up the next day. This was served on a huge family plate and was really popular with the children.

Joe Iafrati's mother always served delicious and nutritious meals even if they were only based on boiled pork bones from Marsh and Baxters' butchers shop or scraps from Smart's the bacon and ham curers. She also made incredible spaghetti dishes served with fluffy potato dumplings and smothered in home-made tomato sauce. His father was an expert sausage maker who would salt and cure the ham in open trays which were left in the pantry. He would put the ham through a mincer and then stuff it into the skin from the intestine of a sheep, which had been purchased from Smarts, and by this method formed his sausages. The sausages were then hung on a long pole, which stood in the corner of the kitchen. There they would remain for months while pieces were cut off, a length at a time, as an accompaniment to the spaghetti. Parmesan cheese was purchased in blocks sometimes being brought back after visits to Italy. Cheese would be grated from the block, as and when required, and it was not unusual for the block to last up to two years.

The DeFelice's shop, a real culinary emporium, complete with resident monkey stocked lubines. These were flat beans with stalks sticking out of the sides and were kept in buckets of cold water. When the shell was removed the bean inside was a real delicacy. Joe Mattiello recalls that 'You could go and buy a pen'th or ha' p'th and they would put them in newpaper like chips and you sort of bite them and press them out of their skin'. Joe Iafrati remembers being told that the bean was reputed to have grown in the desert at the time of Christ. When Christ wandered in the wilderness for 40 days the Devil came looking for him and hid behind the bean plants. However, the wind blew and the beans rattled and the hiding place was discovered. This betrayal was not forgotten, or forgiven, and forever people would eat the beans without getting full as a punishment to ... the beans.

Many of the Italians recalled shopping in the Bull Ring late on Saturday afternoons looking for cut-price bargains; the excitement of bidding at the meat auctions and the feeling of elation at getting a 'good buy'. Liptons would sell the bacon off-cuts so necessary for tasty pasta sauces and also cracked eggs which were used up so quickly in ice-cream making. The fish stall on the Market Hall steps always had a crowd around late on a Saturday, eager to purchase perrywinkles (with a pin) at 2d (1p) for a cornet bag. The better-off bargain hunter was able to procure shrimps and prawns in 3d (1fip) and 6d (3p) bags, which they dipped into on the way home. If, by any wonderous chance, there was any money left, this would be spent on a 6d (3p) huge bag of broken biscuits from Pattisons which, to the infant shopper, was luxury indeed.

Pat Houghton remembers well the many heated arguments that raged between her and her friends, who insisted that Italians 'ate worms'. Macaroni was never included in an English diet and the children earnestly believed that this was what it was. She also remembers getting her own back on one friend when she discovered that her family cooked their sausages by poaching them in milk. 'You think that we are funny' she remembers shouting triumphantly. One evening, when she was fed up with the children's taunts Pat brought them all into her house to watch her father eat his pasta. It was his first meal of the day and he told the wide-eyed children that it was really tomorrow's breakfast and he was saving time by eating it that night!

There were several leading Italian retailers in the St Bartholomew's District. The Ferrarin family stocked all manner of Italian foodstuffs, the Bastianellis originally ran a tobacconist's shop but also stocked popular necessities. Maria Tersigne used to buy her three pen'worth of sweets there, which she was allowed after church on Sunday. The Devoti's home-made sweet shop was filled with mouth-watering delicacies. The Tavolier's worked hard in their fish and chip shop where there was always a long queue of hungry residents

CINI BROTHERS & CO
LIMITED

Wholesale Wine & Spirit Shippers and Importers

Head Office:

37 THE HIGHWAY, LONDON DOCK
LONDON, E.1

Telephone: ROYAL 6237/6238

Telegrams: Cinibrovin, Edo, London

Cellars: 8 Neptune Street, London, E.1

October 1937

Courtesy of J Iafrati   Cini Brothers price list, October

Photograph courtesy of J Sartori/M Giansante

Tavolier's shop, Duddeston Road

on a Friday night waiting to purchase their fish and chip suppers. Most Italians families made their own supply of highly potent chianti in the family brewhouse and this was brought out at any excuse.

The Saracines ran a coffee shop at 109 Coleshill Street. Giuseppi and Maria had five children, Louise, Celeste, Teresa, Maria and John. Teresa married Giovanni Di Mascio after they met whilst he was a lodger at the café. He had moved from London for a while to work on the terrazzo flooring being laid at the Queen Elizabeth Hospital and Lewis's store. Lyn Di Mascio-Walton described how Giovanni purchased a BSA motorcycle and large sidecar, which he used to fill with grapes from the market in the Bull Ring. These were made into wine in five gallon glass jars and at least five of these were emptied each weekend. When the spaghetti was cooked and ready to be served a red candle was placed as a signal in the window of the café and the customers would flock in for good food, wine and music.

WHOLESALE PRICE LIST No. 4175

Duty paid delivered London or f.o.r. London

★

Italian Wines

	Duty paid per gall.	Duty paid per doz.
SPARKLING WINES		
Asti Spumante, Flli. Fiocca	...	68/-
Asti Spumante, Muscatel, Flli. Gancia	...	72/-
MOSCATO		
"Bosca" and other brands	11/-	36/-
CHIANTI, Red, original, bottled in Italy		
"Fassati" in litre flasks	...	39/6
"Dal Canto" „	8/6	36/-
"Chiarusi" (Rufina)	8/6	35/
"Ricasoli" Brolio, vintage 1933, litre flasks	...	42/-
"Ricasoli" „ 12 × 2 flasks	...	78/-
"Ricasoli" Meleto, litre flasks	...	38/6
"Ruffino" blue capsule	...	45/-
"Ruffino" red „	...	42/-
"Ruffino" green „	...	38/-
CHIANTI, RED, bottled in London		
"Dal Canto" "Chiarusi" (Rufina) etc.	8/6	28/-
CHIANTI, WHITE, original, bottled in Italy		
"Ricasoli" Val D'Arbia, litre flasks, vintage 1934		39/-
ORVIETO WINES,		
Mellow (Abbocato) or Dry (Secco), in Orvietan flasks	...	36/-

Courtesy of J Iafrati   Extract, Cini Brothers price list, 1937

Teresa Saracine used to push a large handcart to the Bull Ring market on Wednesdays and Saturdays, which she would fill with 12 huge cabbages or cauliflowers, 4 large bags of potatoes, and apples and oranges. She did all the cooking at the café and she also provided years of free meals for the poorest Italian and English families who attended the school or church. Lyn goes on to say that "Teresa was as good as any Salvation Army kitchen. She helped most families in the Italian Quarter in the same way".

Whilst pasta and pizza have become integrated into the English diet it is interesting to note that no reciprocity in the form of fish and chips has been established in Italy!

Courtesy of T Barlone   Death announcement card, J Barlone

Chapter 5

One big happy family

We was never bored as children". (Harry Zacaroli)

As already shown the Italian Quarter developed in an area where there was plenty of cheap accommodation with easy access to the places of entertainment where the Italian musicians and street-sellers plied their trade. New arrivals knew they would find an existing Catholic community, served by St Michaels Church, and plenty of their fellow compatriots.

Like their English counterparts from a rural background, the Italians:

> Had few skills for industrial employment, and so had to settle close to sources of unskilled and irregular work.....like them too, they could afford only the cheapest form of housing. In common with the English poor, they sought protection and mutual support by living amongst their kin [Chinn, 1994].

Research by Sponza and Green shows that this was also the case in London's Italian Community and that of Manchester grew in the Ancoats District, close to the markets and places of entertainment. As far as South Wales was concerned Colin Hughes' research has found:

> The importance of family life, concentration on the successful running of a business, a limited opportunity for leisure activities and continuing contact with Bardi were all typical aspects of Italian life in Wales in the first half of this century.

The regional alliances remained very strong amidst Birmingham's Italian community, reinforced by their shared native tongue - *Noblidani*. Although some descendents later learned to speak Italian it bore little resemblance to the language spoken by their forebears. One person suggested that it was like comparing "Brummie" to standard "Oxford English".

The communal living which was common amongst the early settlers was described in an article entitled The Tramps Hotel published in Birmingham Local Sketches c1879-80:

> Finally, we have a look at one of the houses where the children of the sunny South cling together in their musical expatriation. There is a crucifix over the mantel piece, and one of the walls is covered with small prints of Italian patriots. Otherwise the place looks very much like the others, and the lodgers look very much the same asleep as the other sleepers we have seen. There are only two married couples amongst them, for the institution of lodging house marriage amongst Italians has been necessarily interfered with by the authorities. Some of the Italian wives were far too young to live in these places, and most of them have gone to live in private houses, where they are out of the reach of too exacting officialdom.

In the early nineteenth century the district which became the Italian Quarter had comprised of fairly substantial homes but, as industries and the canal and railway system infiltrated the area, its more prosperous inhabitants moved out, so that by the time the Italians arrived much of the existing property was in a run-down condition. The rates books of Duddeston Row and Bartholomew Street of 1901 list twenty two householders with Italian names mostly living in the back-to-back houses of these streets, but the rates books of 1915 show 55 such householders most of whom are described as being in 'front houses', often with outbuildings and workshops attached - a further indication of the consolidation of the community.

In June 1915, the Birmingham Daily Mail estimated that the number of Italians in Birmingham was between 600 and 700, but evidence from the Aliens Registers would suggest that this was a conservative estimate, possibly counting only persons born in Italy and not taking into account children. On the first of October 1927, the same paper put the number of 'real Italians' at 400 "with another 1,000 on whom the Italian government has no claim".

The close proximity of kin within the Italian Quarter gave it a 'family' atmosphere according to many residents and those not related by blood or by marriage often acted as godparents to each others' children - as with the Zacaroli and Volante families in the first quarter of this century.

Everybody knew everybody in the Quarter and, some sixty years on, Joe Mattiello is able to describe the properties and their occupants. The map of Bartholomew Street with the accompanying list of residents and businesses has been compiled from information given by former residents, complemented by reference to rates books and electoral registers.

Different types and sizes of house were available in the Italian Quarter with varying rents and rates paid according to location, condition and number of rooms. Many of the properties were owned by a single landlord and the arrangement by which young married couples lived in the parental home usually ensured that the property remained in the same family for at least a couple of generations.

Concern about much of the property in the area was expressed as early as the turn of the twentieth century when extensive enquiries were made into the condition of houses in the Floodgate Street area. It was in the early 1930s that the demolition workers set about flattening the houses which had for almost a hundred years been the homes of Birmingham's Italian settlers.

Marsh and Baxter's abattoir on nearby Chapel Street provided a focal point for much of the daily activity in the district of St Bartholomew's.

The fun really started when a few pigs escaped from their drover whilst being herded along the streets. They would rampage down the main street bringing mayhem to the shop displays and terror to unwary shoppers. Gangs of young boys would encourage the animals by loudly cheering the beast's escape bid right into the Bull Ring and fruit markets where stalls of fresh produce were wildly demolished. Tom Colleran remembers buying produce for his shop from Jamaica Row and watching an unsuspecting lady shopper languidly checking fruit prior to purchase. Unbeknown to her a very friendly cow, who had nimbly evaded all attempts at capture, lumbered up behind her and nudged her on the shoulder. Throwing her basket of purchases in the air, she flung herself screaming onto an adjacent stall full of eggs which immediately collapsed smashing eggs far and wide. Veronica Holliday lived opposite Marsh and Baxter's as a child and used to peer down the pavement grating to see the blood running along channels before being collected to make into black puddings.

Pigs and their drover
High Street, Deritend (Near the corner of Heath Mill Lane)
September 1903

Just up the road stood Belmont Passage where Nancy Jones well remembers the Munroes who were caretakers of the sheepskin dipping yard. Swarms of flies would descend on the whole area attracted to the skins as they were laid out prior to dipping and thousands of maggots hatched and wriggled in the sunshine, to the great fascination of watching children.

During the long summer evenings the streets were as busy as the daytime and really buzzed with activity. Small children scoured the streets and gutters looking for 'special' stones to play jackstones and pieces of slate for hopscotch. Older boys spent hours swapping cigarette cards amongst one another, poring over them and negotiating sagely for the best swaps. All this happened as the men sat indoors drinking Chianti and playing cards whilst the women sat on their doorsteps chatting in their native tongue. Eileen Kenny (nee Bove) lived on Bartholomew Street and recalls that on Sundays a group of Italian men would gather in the backyard where they would "play cards with barrels of beer, and often ended up with arguments". Once the local factories and railway goods yard had closed for the day John Abbiss recalls:

> Around six or seven o'clock the streets were our playground There were seasons for different games... Cricket .. the lamp post as stumps... Rounders the same lamp post as base. Skipping with the rope anchored by that lamp post. All our dreams and secrets were discussed under that lamp.

Photograph courtesy of B Eastment
Volante family

47

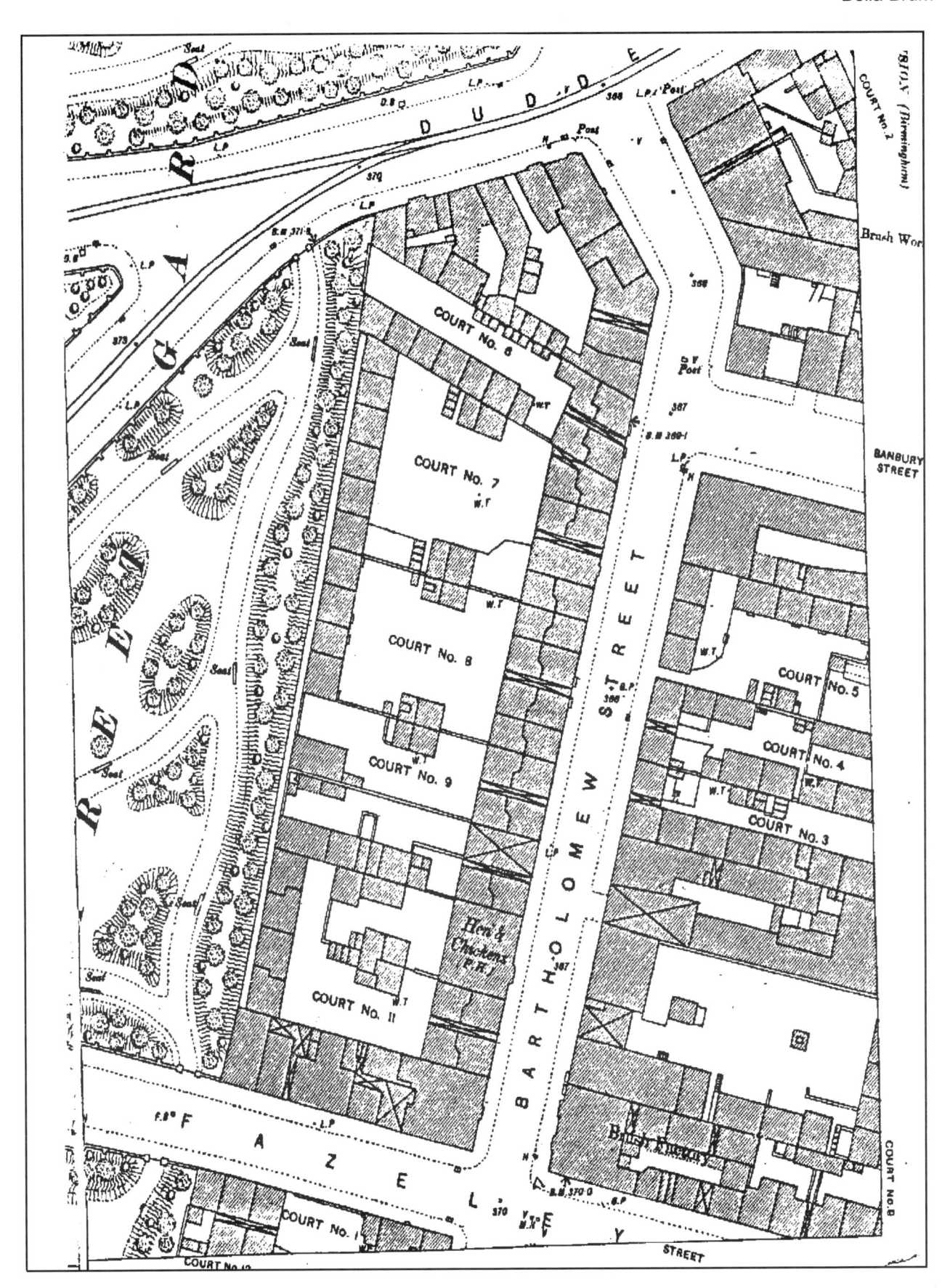

Map of Bartholomew Street

BARTHOLOMEW STREET

HOUSE No	1	MATTIELLO, Guiseppe	Tinsmiths and house
	2	SMITH Arthur "Nigger"	Coal seller
	3	SECONDINI Virgilio	Ice-cream and stores
	4	JONES Wm "Milky Billy"	Milkman
	5	THOMPSON Ann Selina	Coal yard
	6	RAPONI	Bookmakers
COURT No	6	GREEN John Wm	BOVE Ernest
		RICHARDS Wm	[empty]
		FORD Wm	[empty]
		KESTERTON Harry	KESTERTON Lizzie Ann
HOUSE No	7	JENNINGS Mary Ellen	Hucksters shop
	8	TURNER Alfred	
	9	LAVENDER Ellen	
COURT No	7	MANCINI	DAVIS James Wm
		CASINELLI John	HARRISON Wiliam
		MAGAM Enoch	LOMBARDI Peter
		CASTELLUCCI	[2 empty properties]
HOUSE No	10	PICKEN Frank	
	11	FERRARRIN Raffaele	Grocers shop
	12	CATULLO Saverio	Boot & shoe repairer
	13	MARCANTONIO Martin	
COURT No	8	[empty]	BIANCHI Marie Mary
		LAHNNA Ellen Elizabeth	KNOWLES Joseph H
		ARPINO Joseph	HARRISON Emily
		TAMBURRO Philip	RYDER Wm Henry
HOUSE No	14	WASSALL Thomas	
	15	HANCOX Gertrude	
	16	DAVIS Edwin	
COURT No	9	HEALEY John Thos	BROADFIELD Thos
		MOUSLEY Horace	LAHNNA Teresa
		IAFRATE Mark	
HOUSE No	17	[Empty]	
	19	STOKES Henry Frederick J	
	20	COTTERILL Leonard	Shop
	21	[empty]	
	22	VITO Angelina	Dressmaker
COURT No	11	FREZZA Luigi	REA Mary Louisa
		MARGIATTA Phyllis	BARTON Harold Ernest
HOUSE No	23	PHILLIPS Albert Norman	
	24	LAMBERT D	Offices and warehouse

Everyone had a 'whip' but often several children had to share a top and the games were played fiercely from one end of the street to the other. All of the players had a favourite hole in the ground in which to place their top and wails of "mom, she's pinched my hole" resounded all around the courts.

Small girls chalked up hopscotch pitches on the slabs and played until dark when they were made to wash off the marks or "I'll tell your mother". Ropes were left dangling from lamp posts until the next evening as the young swingers were called home to bed.

What a contrast to today when evening finds everyone firmly behind their own locked front doors. Evening then was when the community came together gossiping, joking, drinking and smoking, playing and arguing. No one could possibly be lonely or isolated, everyone knew when a neighbour had a problem. Births were celebrated, deaths were grieved over and everyone had time for their neighbours. Help was extended to all of the people in the area - Italian or otherwise - and Molly Hemmings recalled that when her father had an accident in his coalyard it was their neighbour, Mr Iommi, who carried him across to the house.

But, like all communities, the residents of the St Bartholomew's District had their fair share of neighbourhood disagreements and feuds. One, which reached the courts and was accordingly reported in the local press, took place in 1895 when two Italian families came to blows about a young man who had reputedly been "poached" by one family from the other to work for their family enterprise. Violence erupted when a teacup was thrown at the daughter of the family and resulted in her mother being shot in the leg. Members of the two families later intermarried so the "storm in a teacup" ended happily.

Photograph courtesy of J Sartori — A proud dad and his child

So many young Italians in the area lived with their grand parents that it almost seemed as though a generation was missing. Emotions and feelings were rarely expressed within families and quickly this lesson was learned by the children. For some of the first generation Italians life seemed to be simply transposed from one country to another without too many changes. Large families meant continuity although many babies did not survive infanthood. If women fell ill they rarely called the doctor, begrudging the extra money that this cost, instead treating one another with traditional homeopathic recipes.

Like children everywhere the children in the Italian Quarter formed their own gangs, usually organised by territory - by street or court depending on how many children there were. Joe Mattiello remembers that there was plenty of name calling but very little real trouble. Jeers of "Macaroni Belly" would be countered by retorts of "Fish and Chip Face". The children would forget their differences and run away together laughing when an adult came out and told the children to "clear off and play in your own yard" or "get back to your own end", as remembered by John Abbiss:

ONE BIG HAPPY FAMILY

Photograph courtesy of B Eastment   St Michael's Irish Dance Team,

Photograph courtesy of B Eastment   St Michael's School, Infants Class

Photograph courtesy of F O'Reilly   Zacaroli family

Street fights were often, but by next morning we were all pals again, swopping tales and stories once more on our way to school.

There was never any cheek from the children, they just went home as they knew that back-chatting an adult would lead to more trouble when they got home. Joe Mattiello remembers hordes of children playing the street game 'release' all over the area. The children would divide into two teams. One group would count to 100 whilst the other team hid. They then went in search of them and, when found, the children had to wait in the "den" at the side of a wall. Players who managed to reach the wall without being spotted were able to bang it and shout 'one, two, three release' and were then able to hide again in the next game. The main thrill of ' release' was the enormous area that the game ranged over with players hiding in streets, gardens, parks and cemeteries. Eileen Kenny (nee Bove) recalls the three parks in the area:

> The first one backing onto St Michael's School was called the 'shed park' where football was regularly played, crossing the road in Fazeley Street was the 'flower park' obviously called so for its lawns and flowerbeds and benches. The park on the other side of Albert Street, we as kids, called the 'sand' park simply because of the sand and dust.

When this game palled there was always kicking the can. Joe Mattiello recalls one day in St. Bartholomew's when a crowd of local youths were playing with a can. A group of four or five detectives suddenly pounced as they had been lying in wait for the miscreants. The youngsters fled and were hotly persued by the detectives. One of Joe's friends managed to make it to his his sister's house and actually hid under her bed to avoid arrest ... and all for kicking a can. Ray Zacaroli remembers how the police would also try to catch children playing the popular tip cat game and immediately arrest them. Ray has happy memories of long summer days playing around Curzon Street Station. One day whilst playing with his friend, Tony Miele, Tony found a huge dead rat. He tied it to the back of his bike with a rope and rode up and down the pavement just as the office girls poured out for lunch. Everyone screamed and scattered as the two lads rode off in hysterical laughter .

Most of the people interviewed who were ex-pupils remember St. Michael's School with affection and gratitude to the dedicated teaching staff and some described Miss O'Connor as a strict disciplinarian with a heart of gold. No child dared be a minute late arriving at school as they knew that they would be caned so smartly that their hands would sting all day. Miss O'Connor told the children that if they had been born and lived in Ireland they would have been smacked with a 'slapper' which resembled a cricket bat - so they felt quite privileged at merely being beaten with a cane. Miss O'Connor was an expert at persuading local shop keepers and businessmen to donate gifts to give as prizes to the children. A collection of bikes, prams, scooters and other toys was amassed by this incredible lady which were then given to lucky children.

Photograph courtesy of B Eastment   Class I, St Michael's School, 1930s

The local Member of Parliament, Smedley Crookes was a frequent visitor to the school and Maria Tersigne remembered that Miss O'Connor always managed to obtain cakes and sweets for the children to celebrate his visit - these again donated by local businesses. One little girl had no father and the family was very poor. She fell in love with a beautiful pair of Russian boots worn by Miss O' Connor. The teacher kept the pupil back at the end of the day and insisted that she took the boots as a gift. When Miss O'Connor realised that a child was especially terrified of her she would say to them "What are you afraid of ? I'm not going to kill you, I couldn't stand the blood!" [Beattie Eastment].

St. Michael's Church and School were intertwined in the minds of the children as they both worked closely together. Girls would be auditioned by Miss O'Connor and Miss Barber for the Irish Dance Team. There was fierce competition to become a team member even though the girls were caned if they made any mistake in the dance routine. Miss Barber, the music teacher, chose the members of the choir. Maria Tersigne remembered the Catholic marches, particularly at the Feast of the Assumption, when a statue was carried around the streets and the choir and the dancers performed. However, more than one former pupil remembers being excluded from the procession as a punishment for a minor dismeanour or because they did not have the appropriate clothes to wear.

Pat Houghton remembers the dance troupe performing at the Town Hall on St. Patrick's night with one of the teachers, Miss Curran, dancing a solo. The whole troupe were presented with beautiful silver medals with a gold inlay inscribed and pinned on with a green ribbon. Pat would not take the medal off she was so proud. The following day her father asked her to run round to Barnes' to put on a bet for him. Sadly, the medal fell off and was lost. Pat was heartbroken and although her father tried to get a replacement he was unable to do so.

When the children had to leave St. Michael's and join another school they sometimes ran into childish anti-Italian prejudice from other children to whom they seemed "different". Pat Grego remembers that the boys were always scrapping and name calling - particularly "aye tiddley aye tie, brown bread". During a typhoid scare in the area there was a suggestion that ice cream could be a carrier and Pat punched the nose of a girl who taunted "your dad sells poisonous ice cream".

Photograph courtesy of B Eastment   Having a 'highland' fling

Bella Brum

An alley
Court 6 Bartholomew Street
6 May 1904

Chapter 6

High days and holidays

"We danced the bricks up in the yard" (Madeline Dickson nee Alberici)

If there was one thing that Italian men liked doing it was getting together to socialise. They formed together into what was almost an exclusive men's club meeting up regularly at each other's houses. There they drank chianti and beer from jugs and played cards for money well into the early hours. Interviewees remember that the men were almost fanatical about playing cards and the game became louder and more boisterous as the evening progressed. The women grouped together in the kitchen chatting and producing copious amounts of food which they ferried in to the men throughout the evening. Small boys sneaked under the tables, hidden by the heavy cloths, and picked up and smoked the dropped nub ends of cigarettes. They were also allowed to finish up the left-over food and scrape the saucepans clear of bolognese with the wooden spoons. Some of the lads would have picked up enough of the *Noblidani* language to understand what was being said and to translate it to the other children present. However, on occasions, the interpretation was somewhat loose especially if it involved chores - these would be delegated to the younger children!

Much of the community social life revolved around St Michael's Church which held clubs catering for every member of the family and the community as a whole. The monthly parish magazine paid great attention to every detail of the clubs' activities perhaps trying to persuade others that they were missing something by not joining? Awards and achievements were duly recorded in the magazine and many an Italian child proudly received prizes for continuous attendance at Sunday School.

Vincent Bastianelli ran the Boys Club which was held in an upstairs room at St Michael's. The girls would use an adjoining room to play the piano and practice their dance routines. Father Daley and Sister Anthony would watch closely to ensure that there was no 'hanky panky' between the sexes. The Italian and Irish Catholics shared the church in great harmony and often acted as godparents and witnesses at christenings and weddings. If new parents could not afford elaborate christening gowns for their new babies the church would lend them free of charge.

Beattie Eastment recalls weddings at the Church when almonds would be scattered all over the ground and the children would scamper around the floor picking them up. She was also married at St Michael's where the church was filled with family, friends and neighbours. Her brother Len remembers, as a child, particularly looking forward to eating *crispals* after the wedding ceremony. These were little sugared pastries formed into lovers knots and the children considered them a real delicacy.

Weddings at St Michael's were occasions at which the whole Italian community rejoiced. Houses and yards would be scrupulously scrubbed and long tables set along the whole of the yard. The Tamburro family were always called upon to provide the music and Beattie Eastment as a child, enjoyed dancing to the tune of 'Chitterlings around your hat' - an Italian song with unintelligible words to her!

Jean Thompson's grandfather, Frank Iommi, held parties on a grand scale at his premises on Buck Street, even going as far as to decorate and paint the outside walls of the buildings.

St. Michael's Magazine.

Moor Street, Birmingham.

JANUARY, 1914. PRICE ONE PENNY.

Interior, St. Michael's, Moor Street, BIRMINGHAM.

Meeting of the Men's Guild of the Blessed Sacrament, ... Monday, 9.
" " Young Men's " " " "
" " Girls' Guild, ... Tuesday and Thursday, 8.
" " Mothers' Guild, ...Monday, 8.
" " Children of Mary,... ... ... Sunday, 6.
" " Boys' Guild, ...Every evening at 6-30.
" " Guild of St. Agnes, every evening except Monday, 6-30.
" " League of the Cross, ... Saturday and Sunday, 8.

Printed by S. Walker, Hinckley, Leic.

St Michaels Magazine, 1914

She recalls:

> On special occasions such as weddings, we would use what we called the coach house. This was a long covered arch where there would be one very long table. Christmas time was the best. Our mother and father would take us to grandad's on Christmas Eve where we would eat and drink. I can always remember that there was lots of food, fresh fruit and cases of wine were always sent from Italy.

The Birmingham Evening Despatch of 12 February 1930 carried a description of the wedding of two Birmingham-born Italians. Some sixty years later a relative of one of the bridesmaids, Lyn Di Mascio had her own Italian-style wedding when she married Mark Walton. This included the giving of bridal favours to each lady guest. They consist of a net of five almonds representing health, wealth, happiness, fertility and luck.

When Molly Allchurch married Sid Hemmings at St Martins in the Bull Ring just after the Second World War she vividly remembers coming out of the church door to see "Queenie" (Mrs DeFelice) loudly cheering and waving a string of sausages! This was not some strange form of wedding ritual as Queenie had a stall in the Bull Ring and simply rushed across to the church, still carrying her wares. Eugenio and Eugenia DeFelice were known as "Kingy" and "Queenie" in the St Bartholomew's area, but there are varying accounts about how they came to be so called. Some said it was because they were cousins who married and were reputedly descended from Napoleon Bonaparte whilst others suggest that they were the undisputed leaders of Birmingham's Italian Quarter, having settled there in the last few years of the nineteenth century.

Weddings, funerals and baptisms were huge affairs as many of the Italians of the community were related by blood or marriage and sometimes both! In the towns and villages of the Comino Valley weddings are still occasions for the whole community and the open-air feasting lasts all day and well into the night.

School Matters

While many hearts beat high with joy, many more bumped low with grief, in the Girls School on Friday afternoon, October 30th. On that day the prizewinners of the Scholastic Competitions of the preceeding twelve months walked proudly through the ranks of their school companions to the acompaniment of the plaudits of admiring and perhaps excusably jealous friends, to receive the precious trophies of victory, while others looked on and thought of what, too, might have been their good fortune had they shown the spirit of earnest work, and the . . . proofs of regular attendnce of their rivals.

The Roll of Honour

The folowing were rewarded:-
For Perfect Attendance,
Nellie Woodridge, Ester Sharrock, Kathleen Watson, Marie Sabbato, Mary Thomas, Christine Panicali, Lily Goulding, Lucy Mezzone, Clara Green, Elvira Devoti, Ellen Gibson, Annie Grego.
For Regular attendance
Lizzie Thomas, Louisa Veraca, Ester Devoti, Kate Bacchiochi, Cissie Mitchell, Lily Lumley, Marie Tarantonio, Veronica Mattiucci, Agnes Grady, Teresa Grego, Assunta Arpini, Katie Garghan, Teresa Pollicelli, Elvira Facchini, Jane Wallace, Winifred Woolridge, Rosa Kelly, Cissie Chambers, Winnie Mulligan, Jane Taylor, Annie Canova, Rebbeca Roche, Ellen Watson, Jane Morris, Mary Volante, Yolandi Catulli, Flossie Goulding, Eliz. McCue, Jessie Raisen, Norah Chambers, Lizzie Facchini.

Extract from St Michael's Magazine
Jan 1914

Without exception all of our interviewees mentioned John McCoy with great affection. He came to St Michael's school as a teacher in November 1929, later becoming headmaster. He introduced boxing and football to St Michael's School and Church and ran the sports teams. The boys trained in boxing in the Guildhall and often professionals, such as Spud Murphy, came to visit as a favour to Mr McCoy and to inspire the boys When the boxing champion Primero Carnero visited the Adam and Eve Public House in 1931 he was swamped by young fans. Mr McCoy's arrival at the school was vividly remembered by a former pupil of the school during the period 1929-38:

> The children of St Michael's whose identity up to that point in time had only differed in that their names were generally of Italian or Irish origin, were suddenly given an individuality which had previously been reserved, usually, for the wrong reasons. Now these children were in a school that was beginning to have all its athletic talent marshalled into competing teams. Slowly ... then with roaring crescendo, the name of St Michael's and its talented pupils were something to be conjured with in the world of sporting activities.

Photograph courtesy of B Eastment
Wedding of Beattie Volante

Photograph courtesy of L Di Mascio Walton
Wedding of Lyn Di Mascio

High Days and Holidays

Mr McCoy would give the boys their bus or tram fares if they were playing matches at such places as Perry Barr. He would send them off proudly wearing their school colours. Frank Di Mascio, who was just eight years of age when Mr McCoy came to St Michael's, gave the following testimonial:

> I look back in pride in being one of St Michael's representatives on the football field in a black and white striped jersey which was meant for a much older and larger person but which had, nevertheless been "obtained" through Mr McCoy's endeavours on the team's behalf because funds were not available for our gear.

Joe Mattiello remembers that Mr McCoy would go along to speak to parents and ask them to free their sons up on a Saturday from work so that they could play. Few disagreed with him. Boxing matches were held regularly against such rivals as Kyrle Hall. They enjoyed incredible amenities such as modern premises and a proper gymnasium and the Guildhall boys used to feel rather jealous. Sadly, as they grew older, many of the boys defected to the Kyrle Hall where prizes could be won rather than just trophies, certificates or the honour of winning.

Holidays or day trips to the seaside were very rare amongst the inhabitants of the Italian Quarter although some of the older generation would occasionally return to Italy to visit family. Father Daley and Mr McCoy financed and organised camping holidays for the boys to Ireland and, for many of the lads, this was their first sight of the sea. They would go for a month during the school summer holidays and the trip would provide plenty of tales to be told to family and pals throughout the winter nights. No similar outings were made for the girls at the school and for many of them their first trip on a train occurred when they were being evacuated in 1939 at the start of the Second World War.

ITALIAN WEDDING

Bridal Attendant in Blue at Birmingham Ceremony

An Italian wedding took place at St Michael's Church, Moor Street, Birmingham, today, the parties being Mr Anthony Cappuccitti of 121 Bartholomew Row, and Miss Marie Cibita of back 25 Duddeston Row.

The bride, dressed in the conventional ivory and georgette, carried a bouquet of white lilies and her two sisters, Laura and Hetty, and Louisa Di Mascio (bridesmaids) wore blue silk dresses trimmed with lace, and blue veils to match.

In addition to the bridesmaids the bride was also attended by Mary Grace Cull and the bride's nephew (Master Joseph Grego) both in blue Victorian dress.

Mr and Mrs Cappuccitti afterwards left for London.

Birmingham Evening Despatch   12 Feb 1930

Photograph courtesy of E Kenny   Holywell

The annual pilgrimage to St Winifreds at Holywell on the Feast of the Assumption was the high spot of the Church year. Weekly payments would be collected during the year and Italian residents would board a charabanc outside the church laden with sandwiches, bottles and changes of clothing. The excitement and air of expectation was intense. Maria Tersigne's family went every year, on 15th August although the children had to take it in turns to be part of the party. Everyone attended the St Winifreds Church for mass and then the priest would form a procession with the choirboys to St Winifred's Well. As a child Maria thought that the well resembled a huge swimming pool and she used to watch in awe as the sick were lowered or walked into the freezing water. Joe Iafrati recalls one occasion when he watched four Italian men reverently lowering their mother, fully clothed, in a wheelchair into the water but, to the child's disappointment, she was not instantly cured.

Bella Brum

Photograph courtesy of F O'Reilly

Wedding of Marco Iafrate and Jean Seconini, 5 October 1931

WEDDING RECEPTION OF MARCO IAFRATE AND JEAN SECONDINI
AT THE GRAND HOTEL, COLMORE ROW ON 5 OCTOBER 1931

```
  8    6    4    2    1    3    5    7    9

 10   20                             21   35
      19                             22   34
 11   18                                  33
                                     23
 12                                       32
      17                             24
 13                                  25   31
                                     26
      16                             27
      15
                                     28
                                     29
  14                                      30
```

#	Name	Role
1	Marco IAFRATE	Bridegroom
2	Jean SECONDINI	Bride
3	Christine SECONDINI	Bridesmaid (sister of bride)
4	Jolsomino SECONDINI	Best Man (cousin of bride)
5	Enrico IAFRATE	Father of groom
6	Domenico SECONDINI	Father of bride
7	Elsie MANCINI	Bridesmaid (in-law of bride)
8	Guiseppe IAFRATE	Uncle of groom
9	Maria SECONDINI	Mother of bride
10	Mary MAZZONE	In-law of bride (Newport Pagnall)
11	Miss ARPINO	Family friend (Bedford)
12	Miss ARPINO	Family friend (Bedford)
13	Anthony ARPINO	Family friend (Bedford)
14	Loiusa MAZZONE	In-law of bride (Newport Pagnall)
15	Richard HAYFIELD	Family friend (Newport Pagnall)
16	Michele MAZZONE	Brother-in-law of bride
17	Mrs ARPINO (snr)	Family friend (Bedford)
18	Mr ARPINO (snr)	Family friend (Bedford)
19	Maria POZZUOLI	Family friend
20	Restituta IAFRATE	Aunt of groom (nee FACCHINO)
21	Louisa FACCHINO	Family friend
22	Domenico FACCHINO	Family friend
23	Katie SABBATO	Familiy friend
24	Aida De LUCA	Cousin of bride (nee SECONDINI)
25	Mary De LUCA	Cousin of bride (Watford)
26	Angela De LUCA	Cousin of bride (Watford)
27	Leo Serafino MATURI	Family friend
28	Maria MATURI	Family friend
29	Angelina VITO	Family friend
30	Virgilio SECONDINI	Brother of bride
31	Not known	
32	Not known	
33	Giorgio MAZZONE	In-law of bride
34	La BRIGIDDA	Family friend
35	Angelina SECONDINI	Aunt of bride

Photograph and guest list courtesy of F O'Reilly

Photograph courtesy of M Volante

St Michael's Hiking Club
Clent, 1939

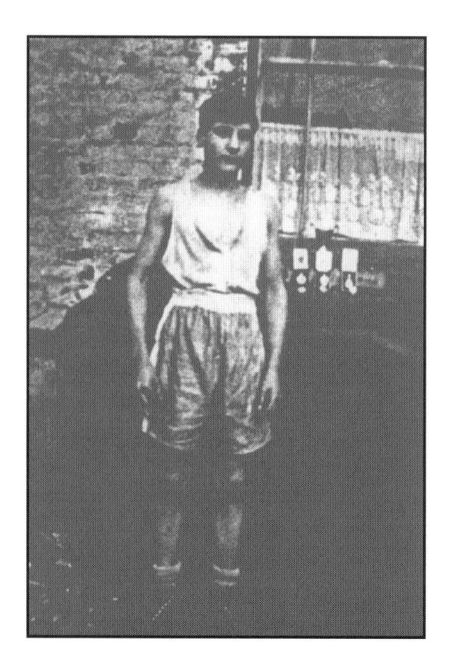

Photograph courtesy of B Eastment
Ernie Volante, with boxing medals

Photograph courtesy of St Michael's Church
St Michael's School Junior Football Team, 1935-36

HIGH DAYS AND HOLIDAYS

Photograph courtesy of M Volante

St Michael's boys about to depart for a holiday in Ireland
Snow Hill Station, 1937

Italians from other communities also made the pilgrimage so it was very much a social occasion as well as a religious one.

Being involved with the ice cream and catering trades, public holidays were usually the busiest times of the year for the Italians and often the whole family was called in to help with ensuring that there was enough to sell. They would often travel as far as the Lickey Hills and other beauty spots where those fortunate enough to have a day off work would congregate. The Onion Fair was another busy time and many a young helper got his (or her) fingers burned or cut as they assisted in the roasting of chestnuts and potatoes.

Some of the Italians continued to use horses as the "pulling power" for their carts well into the 1930s, and Frankie Iommi would dress his horses by plaiting their tails and manes with ribbons and parading them around the local streets.

Celebrations abounded on VE Day and there were street parties across "Little Italy", with everybody "chipping in" with whatever food and drink they could supply. Needless to say, ice-cream was on the menu and the Italian ice-cream makers of the district were renowned for supplying the local schools with free ice-cream for parties. Doreen French (nee Pontone) recalls how her father, Vincenzo, used to provide ice-cream for Nazareth House at Rednal and the Father Hudson's Orphanage at Coleshill.

Bella Brum

Photograph courtesy of V Holliday   Veronica Holliday (nee Lagorio)

Chapter 7

World War II

"Dad came home crying like a baby" (Maria Thompson nee Tersigne)

When Italy declared war on the side of Germany against the Allies, Italians living in Birmingham entered an unpleasant and undeserved period of change. They were bewildered by the changed attitude of both the state and the people as they were suddenly treated with suspicion and avoidance.

Maria Tersigne remembers her father returning from the Bull Ring with his barrow "crying like a baby" on the day that Italy declared war. She recalls that from that day on they were treated like aliens. She was working on the buses, her brother Vincent was in the Army and Tony was in the Navy. Maria's bus went to Nuffield's factory every day after picking up workers for Dunlops. She remembered detectives arriving at their house and confiscating their radio and cameras. Maria shouted at them "But we are British subjects and my two brothers are in the forces", but it did not make any difference, even though the detectives were most apologetic and deeply embarrassed.

Joe Mattiello remembers the financial impact that the war had on the ice-cream makers as there were reduced supplies of ice and sugar needed to make the ice-cream. Pat Houghton recalls having their radio taken from the house and her father put under curfew. None of them could understand why, as both his sons were fighting in the British forces and even his daughter was in the ATS. Pat used to ask her father why he was not 'naturalised'. He would laugh and reply that it cost £12.00p - just think how many pints [of beer] he could get for that!

Pat was evacuated to Retford, Nottinghamshire, in 1940 with her brother Terry. Upon arrival she remembers all of the children being chosen and taken away to homes until just her and Terry were left. In the end the headmaster of the school where the allocation was taking place had to take them home. They were put into a bed that was so large they had to climb a ladder in order to get in and which had crisp, white cotton sheets, a bedspread and two stone hot water bottles. The headmaster's wife asked them if they wanted to use 'the jerry', but they refused as neither of them knew what it was. The next day they went to another home where they were most unhappy, even though they were surrounded by most of the evacuated children from St Michael's School. Pat's father soon arrived and took his unhappy children back to Birmingham. A stonemason who had the yard behind their home had prisoners of war working for him. Pat and Terry would watch them over the wall and listen to them singing. They were unfailingly kind to the children, especially one they called 'Omo', like the soap powder, as he had prematurely white hair and who, obviously, missed his own children back home in Italy.

Mr Zacaroli was arrested under section 18B of The Emergency Powers Act, in the street on his way back home from work. As he walked up Buck Street to Coleshill Street he was met by two detectives and taken home to pack his things. He was taken to Winson Green [prison] and then moved, via Brixton, to Yorkshire where he was interned from June 1940 until December 1941. Only four youths aged 17 years from the Italian Quarter were interned -Norman Phillips (whose mother was Italian), 'Buzzer' Lancer, Ernest Musticone and Pasquali Zacaroli. There never seemed to be any particular reason why these four lads were chosen. Pasquali was a very gentle youth and his desperate mother approached the local Member of Parliament, Smedley Crooke, to try to obtain his release.

Ray Zacaroli remembers his father, Nicoli, being interned at Douglas on the Isle of Man. His elder sister, Elvira [Vera], had married Arthur Connell and was expecting their first baby. When their son was born on 22nd December 1941 she was told that her father was being released. She was so thrilled that she named her son Douglas.

MI5 selected internees to be sent to the Isle of Man. On 30th June 1940 a further selection began but these men were transported to Liverpool docks to board the 1,500 ton liner Arandora Star sailing to Canada.

Tragically the ship was torpedoed on 2nd July 1940, the day after it set on its journey. The German vessel responsible, U47, had previously destroyed the Ark Royal in Scapa Flow in October 1939. Over 700 lives were lost as the Arandora Star sank within 30 minutes, 446 of them being Italian internees. When the news broke in Britain, frantic families desperately tried to find news of relatives. No-one could understand why the ship, which was flying a swastika to denote that it was carrying prisoners of war, should have been attacked. The ship did not have an escort and it carried not only Italians but also German prisoners of war and German Jewish refugees along with British soldiers and anti-submarine guns. It sustained a direct hit on her starboard side which blew up her engine room and plunged the ship into darkness. The majority of the Italians were situated in the bottom deck cabins and most casualties were found in this area. Survivors of the wreck told of the chaos that ensued after the boat was hit. Nicola Cua remembers that there were not enough lifeboats and the cork lifejackets were difficult to use correctly. Ramola Chioccani recalls that the young German prisoners of war, all seamen, seemed to know what to do in an emergency whereas the Italians tried their best but were at a disadvantage, most of them being middle aged and dressed in heavy clothing.

In the aftermath of the tragedy it was discovered that no-one knew exactly how many internees were on the ship or their nationality. One estimate was that 1564 men were on board, between 712 and 734 of them being Italian. The confusion was made worse by the fact that some Italians had swapped papers in order to keep family groups together. Guiseppe Gazzano had been ordered to board the Arandora Star but had given his ticket to a father whose 16 year old son was sailing on it and who wished to stay with him. Changes such as this were not documented, Vincent Pontone's place being taken by Domenico Pontone from Hartlepool.

> **ITALIAN ROUND-UP**
>
> **SWIFT ACTION BY POLICE**
>
> **VIOLENT SCENES IN MANY PARTS**
>
> **EARLY MOVES IN BIRMINGHAM**
>
> The big round-up of Italians has continued unceasingly since Mussolini's declaration of war last evening. Police in London and the provinces have been engaged in an exhaustive comb-out and in many parts violent scenes occured when crowds showed their anger at Italy's action. Rioting broke out, shop windows were broken and many premises damaged.
>
> Many Italians have also been arrested or interned in Australia, New Zealand, South Africa, Southern Rhodesia, India and Cyprus
>
> Swift and effective steps have been taken in Birmingham, but no demonstrations have occured. There are about 200 Italians living in the city.

The internment camps on the Isle of Man were mainly terraced streets of boarding houses and large family properties surrounded by barbed wire fences. Joe Mattiello remembers that his father Guiseppe was interned on the Isle of Man whilst Joe and his brothers were serving British soldiers and his sisters were also involved in war work. The family petitioned for the release of his father who was most indignant at being brought home as he was enjoying himself so much.

Beattie Eastment's father was not interned but his wireless was confiscated and he was put on a 7pm curfew. The police were under orders to check that he was keeping to the curfew and would drop in to chat during long summer evenings. Both her father and mother were forbidden to travel more than a three mile radius from their home, a fact that particularly irked her mother who was a born and bred "Brummie". The situation was made even worse when the children were evacuated to Retford and neither Beattie's father or mother were able to travel to visit them. They were, therefore, unaware when the children were cruelly treated by their foster parents. The children's letters were opened and read and, if they contained any complaints, they were destroyed. When the restrictions were dropped Beattie's mother was allowed to visit them and she brought them straight back home. Beattie's mother was particularly angry that the teachers accompanying her children had not checked upon their welfare. The children remember the feeling of total relief when they finally arrived home.

Pat Houghton remembers that the police regularly visited her home and would search the house from attic to cellar, all in vain, looking for a shortwave radio. Then her father would sit them down, with a cup of tea and a dish of spaghetti, and tell them knowingly "This is all you've really come for!". He enjoyed playing the most wicked tricks on them. When he thought they were due to visit and make a search he would order a ton of coal because they would have to move every piece! In the end they would simply say 'Give us something to eat and we'll go'. As the war progressed the police would call at odd times, often 2am in the morning to check that her father was in. He used to wake one of the children and tell them to lock up when the police had left. He never resented the calls and Pat thinks that he used to actually enjoy the chats with the police as they got to know each other.

The advent of the war meant that the return of the children who had been holidaying in Italy was delayed. Some Italians, fearing reprisals, returned to Italy and British-born sons of Italians were ordered to choose either Italian or British nationality by the age of 21 years. The Italian authorities, for reasons of their own, encouraged the boys to delay their decision. Between 10th and 12th June 1940 when war was declared, anti-Italian protests and riots occured throughout the United Kingdom. Italian shop windows were smashed and looting took place but there was no clear pattern to the violence. It seemed to relate more to local issues, such as unemployment, rather than to Italy entering the war. The internment of Italians started on 10th June 1940 following that of Germans and Austrians. MI5 listed 1,500 'dangerous' names, mostly supporters of the fascist regime but many of these had already left Britain or, like diplomats, were immune. Internment related to all Italian males between the ages of 16 and 70 years unless they had resided in Britain for more than 20 years. Most wives and children carried on family businesses in the absence of their menfolk and many of the young children joined the mass evacuation into the country. Hundreds of Italians were shipped to Canada but, after the tragic sinking of the Arandora Star, there were no further mass evacuations. A mechanism was set up to consider cases for release of internees as by this time 4,000 people had been interned. Some formed the Pioneer Corps, working in areas such as forestry work, but 1,000 remained in internment until the end of the war. Italian prisoners of war (POWs) were also sent to Britain and there were over 150,000 by the end of the war, which was the highest number in any western country. Most of them were sent to work in agriculture because the Geneva Convention prohibited any prisoner undertaking "operations connected with war".

The first POWs arrived in Liverpool in June 1941 and by 1943 70,000 had been dispersed around Britain. They were placed in camps and hostels, on farms and with families. In 1943 The Cabinet decided to release prisoners from the Geneva Convention and employ them, more flexibly in industry and mining. However, they still remained POWs for disciplinary reasons. This decision was not approved by the Italian Government and finally, in April 1944, the POWs were allowed a wage for the work they performed. This could be sent back home to their families in Italy. They were, therefore, still able to act as breadwinners even though they were so far away from home. At the end of the war about 1,400 stayed in Britain as immigrants.

BIRMINGHAM ITALIANS

52 INTERNED, OTHERS TO RE-REGISTER

POLICE STATEMENT

Fifty two Italians left Birmingham by train to be Interned. This leaves a further 150 in the city, who are being registered as enemy aliens.

Last night the Birmingham C.I.D issued an order calling upon all British-born wives of Italians who, since 1933 have been exempt from registration, to go back to the police and register. It was pointed out that these women will be subject to the same restrictions under the Aliens Order as their husbands.

"It must be made perfectly clear to these people", said Superindendent Baguley, "that they are enemy aliens and are subject to the restrictions by Articles 6A (limitation of travel etc.) and 9A (possession of prohibited articles).

He added that among the articles which an enemy alien was prohibited from having in his posssession were motor cars, cameras and wireless apparatus of any kind. In addition they were subject to a curfew.

Extract from the Birmingham Mail
June 13 1940

In common with other Birmingham residents the German air raids took their toll of those living in the Italian Quarter. All recalled with sadness the tragic deaths of the Bastianelli family when Anthony, Carolina and daughter Laura were killed by a direct hit on the Duddeston Row Air Raid Shelter on 28th July 1942.

Schoolchildren, at Aston Station, awaiting evacuation
Birmingham Post, September 2 1939

BASSETT, JANE MARIA, age 86; of 36 Kingston Road, Small Heath. Widow of James Bassett. 19 November 1940, at 36 Kingston Road.

BASTIANELLI, ANTHONY, age 66; of 51 Duddeston Row. Husband of Carolina Bastianelli. 28 July 1942, at Duddeston Row Shelter.

BASTIANELLI, CAROLINA, age 67; of 51 Duddeston Row. Wife of Anthony Bastianelli. 28 July 1942, at Duddeston Row Shelter.

BASTIANELLI, LAURA, age 29; of 51 Duddeston Row. Daughter of Anthony and Carolina Bastianelli. 28 July 1942, at Duddeston Row Shelter.

BATCHELOR, ADA, age 38; of 3 Alfred Street, King's Heath. Wife of George Batchelor. 27 September 1940, at 3 Alfred Street.

Roll of Honour, Birmingham Civilian Dead

Photograph courtesy of B Eastment   Philip Volante, January 1945

Chapter 8

Gone... but not forgotten

"We who followed should have gratitute for the courage, labour, care and honesty of our forebears"
(Joe Iafrati)

What now for the modern descendents of those early settlers from Sora?... What remains of those intrepid young men who left Southern Italy in droves to seek for their fortune in the mean, industrial streets of Birmingham... Collecting blocks of ice in little trollies... helping to stir the ice cream in the brew house and taking part in the street experiences of St. Bartholemews are a million miles away from the lives and experiences of the second generation Brummies.

However, on our travels to research this book we found a keen interest on the part of the new generation to rediscover their Italian - ness. Many of the Italians to whom we spoke happily declared that they naturally cheered on Italian football teams and supported Italian sportsmen at the Olympic Games. The children of immigrants were encouraged as children to become totally English. As they became parents and grandparents themselves many of them undertook to learn the Italian language spoken by their fathers and to visit the lands from which they came. Thay have, without exception, expressed pride in the achievements of their parents and grandparents and have been grateful for the solid structure upon which their own lives have been based. Paolo Tullio in his book, North of Naples, South of Rome, states that :

> Italians value the past and its lessons, they value order, saving money, education and self assessment. The family unit makes much of this possible. Family members have the right to call on other members when they need help but to obtain this right they are also subject to the responsibilities of being a member.

As with most emigrant communities, the education of their children has been of paramount importance, and Italian settlers are no exception. The children and grandchildren were all encouraged to make the most of the educational opportunities open to them.

Many of the families that we visited told us proudly of the achievements of their children. The grandchildren of these itinerant Italian entrepreneurs have became barristers, teachers, company directors, language graduates and owners of their own businesses. Many travel regularly to Sora and its surrounding areas, enjoying the opportunity of explaining to their own children where the roots of their existence began. Little Douglas, the baby named in celebration of the release of his grandfather from internment, has become famous for his knowledge of and expertise in selling "Classic Cars". His brother Kevin is a director of operations at an atomic fuel centre. Another brother, Peter, is employed in the electronics industry after gaining his degree and regularly returns to Italy with his Italian born wife, Lucy.

Everyone we spoke to expressed the wish to see the bravery of their forefathers documented. They offered photographs, anecdotes, certificates and wonderous hospitality. Sunday afternoons will often find small groups exploring the streets of the St Bartholomew's district... pointing out familiar landmarks strolling along the canal bank ... photographing the road signs or just standing and looking and taking in the atmosphere. If they close their eyes they may still feel the excitement and ambience and hear the noise, bustle and childrens laughter that permeated those streets in bygone days. The chimes of the modern ice cream van may not be reminiscent of the handbells and cries of the hokey pokey men and the ice cream may not taste quite as delicious, but ...

The Birmingham Evening Mail, on 30th October 1934, asked 'is it the end of Little Italy?'

> ... Is Birmingham's tiny foreign colony in Bartholomew Street going to be broken up? The ice cream vendors, hot potato merchants, and mosaic workers of the quarter have read with darkening brows of the Government enquiry at the Council House, which seems to spell the doom of the homes they have occupied for years - in some cases a whole lifetime...

Bartholomew Street
Court 6

Three hundred Italians lived in Bartholomew Street and the little streets and alleyways around. They cling together in a compact community, held close by race, language and religion, but not clannish, and continually introducing into their midst English wives and husbands, while the swarms of children growing up are not always dark and vivid, but often between colours or even fair.

The reporter was told by a Roman matron:

> Some of the old people are crying their heart out. They came to Bartholomew Street straight from Italy. This has been their home all the time. They have been transplanted once, but if they are transplanted again they will die, for their roots are so firmly in the soil. Eviction is cruel and inhuman. It will finish these poor old Italian folk.

The Italian Quarter in Birmingham was established around close kinship and friendship networks. It was a community of young, single men with only their nationality and poverty in common in the 1860s. By 1920, it had been transformed into a lively and thriving family neighbourhood. These strong bonds remain among their living descendents. Contrary to the fears of the Italian matron, reported above, the 'poor, old Italian folk' were far from 'finished'

They may be gone but they are certainly not forgotten.

Photograph courtesy of B Eastment
Carmena Domenica Volante

GONE ... BUT NOT FORGOTTEN

Photograph R Hopwood

Italian Quarter in the 1990s

Bibliography & Further Reading

BRITISH PARLIAMENTARY PAPERS
Census of England and Wales
General Reports 1883-94

CHINN, Carl
Birmingham the great working city
Birmingham City Council, 1994, 0709302037

COLPI, Teri
The Italian Factor : The Italian Community in Great Britain
Mainstream Publishing, 1991, 1851583440

FOWLER, Sheila R (ed)
Digbeth and Deritend 1820-1987
Digbeth and Deritend Project, 1986-7

GREEN, David R
Little Italy in Victorian London : Holborn's Italian Community
Camden History Review No 15, 1988

HOLMES, Colin
John Bull's Island
MacMillan, 1988, 0333282108

HUGHES, Colin
Lime, lemon and sarsparilla : The Italian Community of South Wales
1991

SPONZA, Lucio / TOSI Arturo (eds)
Italianist : Supplement number 13 : a century of Italian emigration to Britain 1880s - 1980s : five essays
Italianist, 1993, 022614340

SPONZA, Lucio
Italian immigrants in Nineteenth-century Britain : realities and images
Leicester University Press, 1988

TIMMINS, Samuel
The Birmingham and Midland Hardware District
1865

TULLIO, Paolo
North of Naples, south of Rome
Lilliput Press, 1996, 1874675821